Steven Kleemann

# Human Rights Defenders under Pressure

Steven Kleemann

# Human Rights Defenders under Pressure

## 'Shrinking Space' in Civil Society

With a Foreword by Pablo Pareja-Alcaraz

Tectum Verlag

Steven Kleemann
Human Rights Defenders under Pressure. 'Shrinking Space' in Civil Society

© Tectum – ein Verlag in der Nomos Verlagsgesellschaft, Baden-Baden 2020
ISBN 978-3-8288-4590-9
ePDF 978-3-8288-7652-1

Gesamtverantwortung für Druck und Herstellung:
Nomos Verlagsgesellschaft mbH & Co. KG
Printed in Germany

Alle Rechte vorbehalten

Besuchen Sie uns im Internet
www.tectum-verlag.de

**Bibliografische Informationen der Deutschen Nationalbibliothek**
Die Deutsche Nationalbibliothek verzeichnet diese Publikation
in der Deutschen Nationalbibliografie; detaillierte bibliografische
Angaben sind im Internet über http://dnb.d-nb.de abrufbar.

# Table of Contents

# List of Abbreviations

| | |
|---|---|
| ACHR | American Convention on Human Rights |
| ASEAN | Association of South East Asian States |
| AU | African Union |
| CDCJ | European Committee on Legal Co-operation |
| CEJIL | Centre for Justice and International Law |
| CJ-S-ONG | Group of Specialists on the Legal Status of Non-Governmental Organisations |
| CLR | Centre for Legal Resources |
| CoE | Council of Europe |
| COHOM | Working Party on Human Rights |
| Convention No. 124 | The European Convention on the Recognition of the Legal Personality of International Non-Governmental |
| CSO | Civil Society Organization |
| ECHR | European Convention on Human Rights |
| ECOSOC | Economic and Social Council |
| ECtHR | European Court of Human Rights |
| EHRAC | European Human Rights Advocacy Centre |
| EU | European Union |
| EU Guidelines | European Union Guidelines on Human Rights |
| FRA | European Union Agency for Fundamental Rights |
| FRP | Fundamental Rights Platform |
| G8 | Group of Eight |
| HRD | Human Rights Defender |
| HRD Declaration / UN Declaration | Declaration on the Right and Responsibility of Individuals, Groups and Organs of Society to Promote and Protect Universally Recognized Human Rights and Fundamental |
| IACHR | Inter-American Commission on Human Rights |
| ICCPR | International Covenant on Civil and Political Rights |

| | |
|---|---|
| ICESCR | International Covenant on Economic, Social and Cultural Rights |
| ICNL | International Centre for Not-for-Profit Law |
| IGO | International Governmental Organization |
| IHRL | International Human Rights Law |
| ILO | International Labour Organization |
| KAPA | Kampala Plan of Action |
| NGO | Non-Governmental Organization |
| NHRI | National Human Rights Institution |
| NPO | Nonprofit Organization |
| OAS | Organization of American States |
| ODIHR | OSCE Office for Democratic Institutions and Human Rights |
| OSCE | Organization for Security and Co-operation in Europe |
| OSCE Guidelines | OSCE Guidelines on the Protection of Human Rights defenders |
| PVO | Private Voluntary Organization |
| TSO | Third Sector Organization |
| UDHR | Universal Declaration of Human Rights |
| UIA | Union of International Associations |
| UK | United Kingdom |
| UN | United Nations |
| UNESCO | United Nations Educational, Scientific and Cultural Organization |
| UNGA | United Nations General Assembly |
| UPR | Universal Periodic Review |
| VDO | Voluntary Development Organization |
| Venice Commission | European Commission for Democracy through Law |

# Foreword

The work of human rights defenders aims to improve societies and contribute to peace and democracy. They are advocates for positive change and progress. Human rights defenders are key figures for protection against fundamental rights violations and in the promotion of universal human rights.

2018 marked not only the 70th anniversary of the Universal Declaration of Human Rights, it was also the 20th anniversary of the Declaration on the Right and Responsibility of Individuals, Groups and Organs of Society to Promote and Protect Universally Recognized Human Rights and Fundamental Freedoms (Declaration on Human Rights Defenders). With this Declaration, the term "human rights defender" (HRD) became more common and is today a prevalent notion amongst human rights communities around the globe. There is not simple answer to the question "Who is a human rights defender?". The Declaration on Human Rights Defenders and other relevant regional or national documents conceptualise them largely as anyone who defends and promotes human rights in a peaceful manner. This broad definition leads to a lack of clarity, potentially leaving various actors without of protection. As a result, a scientific examination of the subject is necessary. The following work will begin by focusing squarely on the question of how human rights defenders are defined and, through the analysis undertaken, the exceptionally important work of HRDs will be highlighted.

Unfortunately, throughout the past decade the world has witnessed the imposition of gradual restrictions on the freedoms of human rights defenders (the so called "shrinking space"). These restrictions are not confined to authoritarian countries, where severe violations of human rights are common, but, also in countries where democracy is considered strong. Therefore, it is necessary to address the (growing) constraints that human rights defenders face in all environments, including the limits of existing legal mechanisms and norms to protect their work. While actions and opinions should be open to free and frank debate, many State officials are growingly critical of HRDs. All too frequently, the debate is inappropriately focused on the legitimacy of HRDs themselves, which creates a hostile environment for their work. A dangerous, shrinking space.

While the general conflict between human rights defenders and authoritarian or illiberal regimes is not new and is familiar from contexts where there has been larger scale of repression, recent developments in liberal States are somewhat new. The legal restrictions on the operation of individuals and organizations have risen in recent times. Criminalization of lawful activities, registration laws for non-governmental organizations (NGOs) or the restriction of foreign funding are only some of the ways in which human rights defenders are put under pressure. Threats of violence, actual physical attacks, disappearances and killings of HRDs are the most severe methods.

It becomes clear that, to support the important practical on the ground work of human rights defenders, it is necessary to analyse the general situation and the legal improvement opportunities from an academic perspective.

The following piece of work starts with the broader concepts and categories of civil society and human rights defenders, including the role of NGOs and giving a definition of human rights defenders. Afterwards, the existing international legal framework for the protection of HRDs is examined, with a focus on the European region. The following chapter elucidates the shrinking space phenomena and especially highlights the States crack-down on civil society and HRDs within Europe, setting out the uniqueness of their work in the region. Finally, the identified shortcomings are presented, analysed and confronted.

The content of this Master thesis leaves no doubt as to the author's capacity to convey his ideas in a concise yet nuanced manner. The work proves the author's familiarity with the topic and the existing academic literature. The choice of the European context to illustrate the main argument -the gradual loss of space for the effective defence of human rights- deserves special recognition, for it makes a relevant contribution to current debates that put too much of an emphasis on the situation in countries with feeble democracies or persistent authoritarian practices.

Thus, it is a very timely and interesting Master thesis that addresses the (growing) constraints human rights defenders face in most environments, the potential for change and the limits of existing legal mechanisms and norms to protect their work. A critical and well-informed analysis of the main international and regional instruments used to protect the work of human rights defenders, with emphasis on the case of European region will be of particular interest to the reader. In addition, balanced suggestions are offered that allow for shortcomings to be addressed.

Overall, this is an outstanding piece of work that evidences the author's capacity to conduct independent and rigorous research, as well as his familiarity with the many constraints surrounding the activity of human rights defenders. Alternate avenues and mechanisms are required to improve the situation for human rights defenders. This thesis will explore how this can be achieved – leaving the reader armed with knowledge to change the course of history for human rights defenders.

Pablo Pareja-Alcaraz

Barcelona, 20 October 2020

# 1 Introduction

Human rights are abstract principles developed by human beings and codified in international treaties and declarations. But the addressees are human beings and these rights are also experienced and exercised by human beings. The abstract principles of human rights in such declarations and agreements must be transformed into feasible capabilities to be utilized by human beings.[1] To breathe life into abstract principles, standing up against human rights violations and demanding democracy and equality is not only onerous, it is a dangerous, sometimes life-threatening task. This is the point where civil society and human rights defenders come into play.

Unfortunately, the number of opponents of human rights – authoritarian regimes, illiberal elites and organisations, as well as economic profiteers from human rights violations – has risen within recent years. Human Rights Defenders (hereinafter HRDs) are facing severe threats; their working area and capacity is becoming smaller due to surveillance and restrictive domestic laws targeting them.[2] This issue is called 'shrinking space' and it not only affects HRDs but also civil society in a vast number of countries throughout the world.

The human rights movement is facing fundamentally different challenges than ever before, with some even proclaiming "the endtimes of human rights"[3]. However, this should not be simply taken as given, rather it should encourage human rights proponents to urgently reconsider many of their approaches, extend their outreach and re-evaluate their strategies, while remaining steadfast regarding their fundamental principles.[4]

---

1 *Terto Neto*, Protecting Human Rights Defenders in Latin America, p. ix.

2 *Kinzelbach*, Ohne Demokratie keine Menschenrechte und kein Frieden, Peace Lab 12 January 2017.

3 *Hopgood*, The Endtimes of Human Rights, Ithaca: Cornell University Press, 2013.

4 *Alston*, Human Rights Under Siege, SUR 25 – v.14n.25, p. 268.

The aim of this project is to identify weak points in the legal protection of HRDs and how the issue of 'shrinking space' can be addressed. It is worth investigating how the work of HRDs can be strengthened, especially at a time when more states are taking a step back from human rights or trying to separate human rights and the precept of equality. 2018 is not only the 70th anniversary of the Universal Declaration of Human Rights (UDHR), it is also the 20th anniversary of the Declaration on the Right and Responsibility of Individuals, Groups and Organs of Society to Promote and Protect Universally Recognized Human Rights and Fundamental Freedoms (hereinafter The Declaration on Human Rights Defenders or HRD Declaration). Nevertheless, many people across the world seem to have forgotten what it means to defend human rights and how important they are for our societies.

The initial trigger for further research regarding the interplay between civil society actors and human rights can be found in the UDHR itself, whose preamble states that "*every individual and every organ of society*, [...] shall strive [...] to promote respect for these rights and freedoms and [...] secure their universal and effective recognition and observance".[5] Hence, the link between human rights protection and civil society is already enshrined in the cornerstone of modern international human rights law, the UDHR.

The bulk of the literature on the subject focuses on countries with an already poor human rights situation. However, current developments in (previously) liberal and human rights law-abiding states – including even some EU member states – warrants a new focus on western countries or the so-called "global north," in particular, issues that fall under the umbrella of the European Convention on Human Rights. Against this background, it is appropriate to examine more closely the legal protections afforded to HRDs in these states. This analysis proceeds by defining the relevant terminology, identifying the international legal framework, before analysing the shortcomings of the determined protection mechanisms. This lays the foundation to develop arguments to overcome deficiencies in protections for HRDs, and especially to draw attention to the emerging trend of dismantling democracy in western

5 UN General Assembly, *Universal Declaration of Human Rights*, 10 December 1948, 217 A (III), Preamble; emphasis added.

countries. Worldwide, the first stirrings towards repressive or autocratic regime changes are similar and are becoming apparent in countries in the global north. Thus, lessons can be learned both from states and regions where democratic institutions have long been weak, as well as previously strong democracies where illiberal transformations have taken place.

# 2 Civil Society and Human Rights Defenders: Concepts and Categories

To identify the space in which civil society is able to act, it is necessary to define several concepts: 'human rights defenders', 'non-governmental organizations' (NGOs) and even 'civil society' itself must be classified with regard to international law, including civil society's role in shaping human rights law and its implementation. Both the terms non-governmental organization and civil society are each notoriously difficult to define and therefore it is essential to elucidate their application and how the two concepts cohere.[6] After defining these terms, 'human rights defender' (HRD), as a somewhat controversial label, needs further examination and must, for the purpose of this thesis[7], be viewed in the context of civil society and the legal sphere in which NGOs operate.

## 2.1 Civil Society and its Role in Shaping International Human Rights Law

The concept of civil society is highly debated and open to frequently conflicting exegeses.[8] Often, the debate starts from the very definition of the term 'civil society', in terms of the type of activities, groups, structures and realities the term covers and how they affect global governance.[9] Some academics and practitioners in this field consider civil

---

6 *Carew*, NGOs, Political Protest, and Civil Society, p. 11.

7 This volume is based on my IHL master thesis, "Legal Protection of Human Rights Defenders Under International Law - 'Shrinking Space' in Civil Society", 2019, European University Viadrina.

8 *Scholte*, Relations with Civil Society, in: *Katz Cogan / Hurd / Johnstone* (eds.), The Oxford Handbook of International Organizations, p. 713.

9 Ibid.

society synonymous with NGOs.[10] This simplified depiction, however, leaves out many civil society actors who also have essential leverage on the community and governance. Using the terms synonymously would mean that civil society is limited to an association of "formally structured, legally registered, and professionally staffed organizations outside official and commercial sectors that undertake a variety of advocacy and service delivery operations."[11] This is certainly the civil society reflected by Amnesty International, Oxfam, International Rescue Committee, Global Policy Forum, Global Rights or Human Rights Watch or other similar organizations, but such a narrow interpretation does not cover more loosely organized social movements, grassroots movements, nor faith groups, labour unions or employer and industry associations, among many others.[12] Therefore, an alternative definition focuses less on organizations' structure, defining civil society as "a political space where associations of citizens seek, from outside political parties [and, by extension, government], to shape societal rules."[13] This definition is broad enough to cover all respective actors in demarcation to only NGOs and narrow enough to exclude solely political parties or governments. However, this conceptualization is, and should not be limited to only western, liberal or modern societies, and neither does it say anything about ideological, religious or political views. It is also not inevitably 'civil', since the realm of space can be filled with arrogant, violent, racially-prejudiced or discriminating people. For instance, the Mafia, the Ku Klux Klan and other radical and racial groups inhabit civil society.[14] Hence, civil society is an extremely broad concept, which, as Michael Edward defines it, contains

> *"all associations and networks between the family and the state in which membership and activities are 'voluntary' – formally registered NGOs of many different kinds, labor unions, political parties, churches and other religious groups, professional and business associations, community and self-help groups, social movements and the independent media"*[15]

---

10 *Scholte*, Relations with Civil Society, in: *Katz Cogan / Hurd / Johnstone* (eds.), The Oxford Handbook of International Organizations, p. 713.

11 Ibid.

12 Ibid.

13 Ibid.

14 Ibid.

15 *Edwards*, Civil Society, p. 19.

Thus, some define the term as referring to the rule of law, democracy and a human rights-based society, while others consider it constituted by formal and informal groups which may or may not be freely joined by citizens.[16] This approach differentiates civil society from the state and family.[17] Notwithstanding the identified breadth of both the definition as well as the implementation of the concept, the approach of this thesis will be to focus on the role of civil society in shaping human rights policy and law in the global context.

The role of civil society organizations on the domestic and international level is exceptionally important for the development, protection and promotion of fundamental human rights and freedoms. They can – due to their flexibility and structure – deal with more specific themes than administrations or other international institutions.[18] All the more alarming are recent developments in formally liberal and democratic countries. All around the globe, activists, social justice organizations, Human Rights Defenders and nearly everyone who challenges the status quo in a given country face an increasingly repressive environment.[19] "A new era of restricted freedoms and increased governmental control"[20] is enunciated by the World Economic Forum's Global Risk Report. Freedom of association, assembly and expression are most likely to be threatened, especially where populists increase and gain power, and their severe impact on human rights becomes evident.[21] Hence, the problem is widely known and documented. While the issue has reached global proportions, various governments employ different

16 *Van Veen*, Civil Society in Europe and the European Convention on Human Rights, in: *Van der Ploeg / Van Veen / Versteegh* (eds.), Civil Society in Europe: Minimum Norms and Optimum Conditions of its Regulation, p. 3 f.

17 Ibid.

18 *Bourke*, The Role of NGOs in the International Human Rights System: A Case Study—IJM in Thailand, Global Tides, Vol. 4, Article 2, p. 3.

19 *Hayes, et al.*, On "shrinking space" – a framing paper, *Twomey* (ed.), Transnational Institute, 2017, p. 3.

20 World Economic Forum, Global Risks Report 2017, p.29.

21 *Bustos*, The Shrinking of Civic Spaces: What is Happening and What Can We Do? Dejustica, 17 April 2017, https://www.dejusticia.org/en/column/the-shrinking-of-civic-spaces-what-is-happening-and-what-can-we-do/; see further: Human Rights Watch, World Report 2017, *Roth*, Essay: The Dangerous Rise of Populism, pp. 1 ff.

methods to suppress civil society, and thus make it difficult to detect and certainly difficult to combat.[22]

In Europe, civil society NGOs, and especially human rights NGOs, are the main actors in shaping international human rights law among non-state actors. These NGOs and the space, within which they can work, are the focus of this thesis and are analysed in the following section.

### 2.1.1 Civil Society in Europe

Since the project's focus lies on issues and situations under the umbrella of the ECHR, it is worth examining the specific contours of civil society in Europe. However, due to limited space and the scope of the thesis, a more encompassing analysis of the in-depth historical emergence of Europe's civil society will be dispensed with.

In 2012, the EU was awarded the Nobel Peace Prize for its continuous contribution "to the advancement of peace and reconciliation, democracy and human rights in Europe."[23] This evolution from a 'continent of war' into a 'continent of peace'[24] has not, however, been without difficulty. The Euro-crisis, which caused a heavy socioeconomic burden and the resulting political unrest and emerging populism within Europe subsequently warrants concern about human rights on the continent. Nevertheless, the awarded prize highlights the EU's accomplishments and should be understood as a further challenge to emphasise the promotion of democracy, peace-building and primarily, the defence of human rights. What can be deduced from this is the outstanding achievement that can be attained through a vital civil society, the importance strengthening it and the need to resist political impulses that seek to suppress civil society actors critical of the state. As embedded in Article 10 of the EU Lisbon Treaty, "[t]he functioning of the Union shall be founded on representative democracy," and the atten-

22 *Bustos*, The Shrinking of Civic Spaces: What is Happening and What Can We Do? Dejustica, 17 April 2017, https://www.dejusticia.org/en/column/the-shrinking-of-civic-spaces-what-is-happening-and-what-can-we-do/.

23 The Nobel Peace Prize 2012, https://www.nobelprize.org/prizes/peace/2012/summary/.

24 Ibid.

tion paid to the great importance of civil society in Article 11 of the 2009 EU Lisbon Treaty shows the value and importance of civil society inclusion in EU governance.[25] Specifically, civil society organizations can play essential watchdog and collocutor roles in the encouragement of respect for human rights in Europe not attainable through individual citizen engagement.[26]

Civil society organizations are involved with institutions responsible for shaping human rights within the pan-European space in different ways.[27] For instance, the EU and the Council of Europe (CoE) offer wide-ranging, regular, institutionalized and in-depth opportunities for CSOs to influence legislation, whereas the Organisation for Security and Co-operation in Europe (OSCE) involves them in a less binding manner.[28] For example, the OSCE embeds CSOs through interactive conferences allowing an open debate for "dynamic norm-creating process[es],"[29] which, however, might be less appropriate for the actual elaboration and realization of agreed norms, since states and CSOs have frequently deviating views.[30] The CoE consolidates participation of CSOs through its own Conference of International Non-Governmental Organizations, involving more than 400 'participatory status' granted CSOs, providing expert knowledge on rights issues.[31] The Conference is granted a permanent status in the CoE's four governing pillars, or so-called 'quadrilogue'.[32] This status gives the Conference, and hence, civil society, not only the power to set the agenda and provide input on the CoE's work, but it is also thereby awarded official institutional status within the Council.[33] The CoE as an international organization can – through its cooperation mechanism between civil society and its core institutions – be designated as highly inclusive.[34] The most effective mechanism and strongest instrument to empower civil

25 *Thiel*, European Civil Society and Human Rights Advocacy, p. 2.
26 Ibid.
27 Ibid, p. 10.
28 Ibid.
29 OSCE, Human Dimension Commitments 2005, p. xxi.
30 *Thiel*, European Civil Society and Human Rights Advocacy, p. 11.
31 Ibid, p. 13.
32 Ibid.
33 Ibid.
34 Ibid.

society within Europe is certainly the European Convention on Human Rights (ECHR). That ratification of the ECHR is a precondition for becoming a party to the ECHR for membership in the CoE reflects a strong commitment in respect of protecting human rights. Since judgements of the European Court of Human Rights (ECtHR), unlike most other human rights treaty-based bodies, are binding for all member countries, its credibility concerning genuine fundamental rights protection is very high. Furthermore, the possibility for individuals and – for this context, especially important – NGOs to bring claims before the Court, illustrates the great importance of civil society for the CoE and its member states. That NGOs may complain directly before the ECtHR highlights the foundational connection between civil society and legal and normative developments in Europe.[35]

Consistently, the strength of the legal regulatory framework protecting basic rights and freedoms is a benchmark for whether civil society is functioning.[36] In the case of Europe, one can say that a distinctive normative approach towards civil society has emerged.[37] The European Union, the Council of Europe, the European Court of Human Rights and the European Court of Justice set the relevant norms and interpret their substance. However, the coexistence of an abundance of organisations addressing human rights issues does not only mean cooperation and coordination, but rather also entails overlap, competition or even internal conflict.[38] Further, it is worth mentioning the Fundamental Rights Agency (FRA) in the context of civil society and challenges working on human rights.

35 *Van Veen*, Civil Society in Europe and the European Convention on Human Rights, in: *Van der Ploeg / Van Veen / Versteegh* (eds.), Civil Society in Europe: Minimum Norms and Optimum Conditions of its Regulation, p. 9.

36 Ibid, p. 8.

37 Ibid, p. 5.

38 *Thiel*, European Civil Society and Human Rights Advocacy, p. 15.

### 2.1.2 The European Union Agency for Fundamental Rights

Within the European regional framework and the role of civil society within it, the European Union Agency for Fundamental Rights is worth briefly reviewing.

The European Council considered it reasonable to further strengthen and develop fundamental rights through a European agency. Therefore, in December 2003, the Member States passed a resolution according to which the former European Monitoring Centre for Racism and Xenophobia would expand its mandate to fundamental rights in general and transform into an agency for fundamental rights.[39] After a controversial dialogue process regarding the exact competencies of the newly created FRA, the agency was finally established on 15 February 2007 by adoption of Council Regulation (EC) No 168/2007.[40] The identified objective of the new agency is to give Member States and Community bodies the requisite resources to put them in the position to develop policies and implement measures in order to comply with their commitments to preserve fundamental rights.[41] The agency is supposed to be an interface which facilitates the relationship between various stakeholders in the diverse fundamental rights, enables the development of synergies and encourages dialogue among all parties concerned.[42] The FRA functionally represents the assimilation of the EU Charter of Fundamental Rights into the political and juridical scope of the Union.[43] However, the FRA has no legal or enforcement prerogatives but actually operates as consultative and review body.[44] The various stakeholders the FRA is connected with or maintains especially close relationships with are: the Council of the European Union, the European Commission and the European Parliament; other international organizations like the OSCE, the UN and the CoE; as well as

39 *Callies*, The Charter of Fundamental Rights of the European Union, in: *Ehlers* (ed.), European Fundamental Rights and Freedoms, p. 538.

40 *Groenleer*, The Autonomy of European Union Agencies, p. 249.

41 *Callies*, The Charter of Fundamental Rights of the European Union, in: *Ehlers* (ed.), European Fundamental Rights and Freedoms, p. 538.

42 Ibid.

43 *Thiel*, European Civil Society and Human Rights Advocacy, p. 46.

44 Ibid, p. 47.

governments, National Human Rights Institutions (NHRIs), academic institutions, equality bodies and, as one of its main partners, civil society organisations.[45] For the purpose of this thesis, the latter group, civil society organizations, is of particular interest. The close integration of civil society, primarily through NGOs, is again emphasised in paragraph 19 of the founding Council Regulation, where it is stated that:

> *"Recognising the important role of civil society in the protection of fundamental rights, the Agency should promote dialogue with civil society and work closely with non-governmental organisations and with institutions of civil society active in the field of fundamental rights. It should set up a cooperation network called the 'Fundamental Rights Platform' with a view to creating a structured and fruitful dialogue and close cooperation with all relevant stakeholders."*[46]

The inclusion of civil society deploys an incentive structure for the enhancement of EU human rights policies. Through self-amplifying effects, the FRA seeks to assert efficacious influential potential on supranational EU bodies, and together with a strong civil society, presses governmental agencies to respond to its claims. As the structure of future rights regimes shift toward multi-level (state, supranational) governance systems, the question arises as to whether such a transformation achieves a higher degree of respect for fundamental rights as compared to simply relying on national governments to secure these rights.[47] If this is the case, "are non-state efforts by the agency and CSOs sufficiently legitimized when incorporated into supranational governance?"[48] The realization of this 'incorporation approach' should be reached through the already mentioned Fundamental Rights Platform (FRP), as it is the agency's link with civil society. Article 10 of Council Regulation (EC) No 168/2007 provides a list of the Platform's purpose and working methods which are: providing feedback on the FRA's work and annual report; acting as a knowledge pool and mechanism for the exchange of information; being open to all interested and appropriate stakeholders; and also delimiting the FRP's competences

45 Council Regulation (EC) No 168/2007 of 15 February 2007, Chapter 2, Articles 6–10.

46 Ibid, paragraph 19.

47 *Thiel*, European Civil Society and Human Rights Advocacy, pp. 54 f.

48 Ibid, p.55.

when clarifying the Platform's method of operating under the authority of the Director.[49]

Despite the advantages of those new modes of governance, one should bear in mind that CSOs on such a high level are considered to always be representing a 'civic elite'.[50] In the case of human rights organizations, their credibility is of particular importance and therefore all parties involved must act with a high degree of transparency. When the inclusion of CSOs into the FRA's activities meets these demanding requirements, the legitimacy of the Agency and the CSOs is on one hand high, but on the other it exposes them to criticism from governmental actors, especially when politically sensitive outputs are delivered.[51] States might delegitimize the FRA's results by arguing that they are biased, since only particular interests might be pushed through by individual CSOs. This may call into question the EU's achievements, like its self-estimation as the biggest zone of rights, justice, freedom and security realisation worldwide.[52] Thus, it requires a balancing act by the FRA and its Director to respect the various interests of all stakeholders and remain credible and trustworthy, as to fail in this respect could potentially impair the Agency's ability to provide meaningful support for reasonable claims.[53] Despite these possible criticisms, the impact and acceptance of civil society in EU policy making has proven vitally important, and the system's unique approach should provide a model for global governance concepts.

In summary, the normative framework and institutional instruments for the protection and promotion of human rights, as well as the inclusion of civil society in the EU, are at the fore of this field in global comparison. The construction of the FRA and its FRP Platform assimilate civil society representatives, closing the gap between normative-legal improvements resulting from the integration of the Charter of Funda-

49 Council Regulation (EC) No 168/2007 of 15 February 2007, Article 10, paragraphs 1–5.

50 *Thiel*, European Civil Society and the EU Fundamental Rights Agency: Creating Legitimacy through Civil Society Inclusion?, Journal of European Integration, Vol. 36, Issue 5, 2014, p. 444.

51 Ibid, p. 445.

52 Ibid.

53 Ibid.

mental Rights into the European governance structure.[54] Irrespective of the described shortcomings regarding the conceptual and political structure of the agency, the FRP plays a crucial role in making more transparent an otherwise opaque system of European human rights bodies and its success should not only be measured by the results of its work with States, but also by its integration in civil society.[55] Bearing in mind the "legitimizing aspect of participatory EU governance in its human rights policy,"[56] the expectations and outcomes of the FRA's activities may be assessed positively.

## 2.2 Non-Governmental Organizations

While international law is exceptionally diverse, human rights law is one of its key issues. With regard to the United Nations' primary purpose: the maintenance of international peace and security, development of friendly relations among nations, solving inter alia international humanitarian problems and promoting and encouraging respect for human rights and fundamental freedoms[57]; international human rights law (IHRL) is one of the core scopes of the UN and also of the bulk of NGOs. However, only spelling out the provisions of IHRL is not sufficient. Instead, it is necessary to assert such norms to secure an equal rights situation.[58] Not every UN member state is willing or able to enforce the laws upon which they agreed and especially poor or disenfranchised individuals often cannot effectively and straightforwardly claim their rights.[59] At this point, NGOs frequently come into play and intervene on behalf of these persons or groups.[60] Three main methods of intervention can be identified in that regard. First, NGOs can raise public awareness about an issue, in the hope that people will put pres-

54 *Thiel*, European Civil Society and Human Rights Advocacy, p. 66.

55 Ibid.

56 Ibid.

57 Charter of the United Nations, Article 1.

58 *Bourke*, The Role of NGOs in the International Human Rights System: A Case Study—IJM in Thailand, Global Tides, Vol. 4, Article 2, pp. 2 ff.

59 Ibid.

60 Ibid.

sure on the government, also leading to international pressure.[61] Further, human rights violations can be brought before a national court via lawyers working for NGOs.[62] Lastly, NGOs can help people file claims before judicial and quasi-judicial human rights bodes or document a situation and provide crucial information to regional or international organizations such as the EU or the UN, which might then take action with the result that the situation will improve.[63]

After World War II and again after the end of the Cold War, social movements, especially NGOs, became primary actors at the national, transnational and international level.[64] Over time, they took responsibility for intricate, traditionally governmental tasks, for instance "delivering development assistance, mediating social conflicts, setting standards for business, developing expert knowledge, and reconstructing societies after natural and social disasters."[65] They respond to various international problems from climate change to development issues to human rights.

### 2.2.1 Non-Governmental Organizations and their legal Status

While there were social movements before the Second World War, the term Non-Governmental Organization was initially shaped by the UN. Under Chapter X (the economic and social council) in Article 71 of the UN Charter adopted in 1945, it is set out that NGOs can be accredited by the Economic and Social Council (ECOSOC) as participant observers and further they are offered the opportunity to receive consultative status.[66] To grant such status, the UN requests some prerequisites are fulfilled, which are mainly set out by the Union of International Associations (UIA) and laid down in ECOSOC Resolution

61 *Bourke*, The Role of NGOs in the International Human Rights System: A Case Study—IJM in Thailand, Global Tides, Vol. 4, Article 2, p.3.

62 Ibid.

63 Ibid.

64 *Beer / Bartley / Roberts*, NGOs: Between Advocacy, Service Provision and Regulation, in: *Levi-Faur* (ed.),The Oxford Handbook of Governance, p.325.

65 Ibid.

66 *Fowler*, Development NGOs, in: *Edwards* (ed.), The Oxford Handbook of Civil Society, p. 43.

1996/31.[67] Hence, NGOs must, *inter alia*, establish a headquarters with an executive organ and officer with the authority to speak for the members (which shall exercise effective control over policies and actions); a democratically adopted constitution; and independent and transparent funding.[68] The label 'NGO' created in the UN Charter has expanded greatly into a complex and sometimes confusing worldwide discourse far beyond its United Nations origins.[69] For instance, the term 'NGO' was initially applied to organizations working internationally, while nowadays many organisations legally defined as NGOs are domestic.[70] Further, they identify themselves as NGOs whether or not they obtain consultative status or work within an economic and social field. The broader definition evolved *inter alia* through the negative definition approach of 'non-governmental,' which fostered a terminological development that considers "private voluntary organizations (PVOs) in the United States and voluntary development organizations (VDOs) in India; as well as nonprofit organizations (NPOs), third sector organizations (TSOs) and, more recently, civil society organizations (CSOs) worldwide"[71] to have the characteristics of NGOs as initially conceived. Despite the term's expansion and acceptability, or perhaps precisely because of these reasons, there is still no generally accepted definition, nor an undisputed positive classification of what NGOs are, do, or why they occur worldwide.[72] Nevertheless, since 1945, NGOs have been – through Article 71 of the UN Charter – officially recognized in international law.[73] Besides ECOSOC, further international organizations such as the United Nations Educational, Scientific and Cultural Organization (UNESCO), the International Labour Organization (ILO) and various regional organizations like the

67 *Martens*, Examining the (Non-) Status of NGOs in International Law, Indiana Journal of Global Legal Studies, Vol. 10, Issue. 2, Article 1, pp. 16 f.

68 Economic and Social Council, E/RES/1996/31, para. 10–13.

69 *Fowler*, Development NGOs, in: *Edwards* (ed.), The Oxford Handbook of Civil Society, p. 43.

70 Ibid.

71 Ibid.

72 Ibid.

73 *Martens*, Examining the (Non-) Status of NGOs in International Law, Indiana Journal of Global Legal Studies, Vol. 10, Issue 2, Article 1, p. 15.

Organization of American States (OAS) or the Council of Europe have devised official consultative or participatory arrangements for NGOs.[74]

Most NGOs appear on the domestic level and their legal status is defined by the laws of the respective state.[75] Despite many attempts by international lawyers and social scientists to regulate and establish the legal status of NGOs states have not agreed to a treaty clarifying the status of NGOs under international law.[76] Therefore, NGOs are compelled to accept the domestic laws of the state in which they are registered.[77] So, from a juridical perspective, it is worth examining how the legal position of NGOs in the domestic context affects international law. In western societies, the affiliation of people to a societal organisation can be connected to basic civil rights such as freedom of speech and/or freedom of association. However, the elaboration of national laws in that regard differs between various countries and thus the legal situation of NGOs also differs.[78] These circumstances provoke problems when NGOs operate in the international sphere, exceeding the borders of their country of origin and therefore falling under different domestic legal systems.[79] This is the case for NGOs acting internationally with local branches in various states. At the same time, some international governmental organizations (IGOs), such as the UN, require a certain domestic legal status as a prerequisite to apply for 'consultative status', and thus NGOs cannot avoid domestic jurisdiction while also being actively involved at the international level.[80] Consequently, it is necessary to define a legal framework for NGOs. Among all different national legislation, Belgian law provides an instructive example and should be emphasized. It ascribes NGOs operating internationally 'preferential status', although their headquarters are situated outside

74 *Weissbrodt*, Roles and Responsibilities of Non-State Actors, in: *Shelton* (ed.), The Oxford Handbook of International Human Rights Law, p.723.

75 *Wouters / Rossi*, Human Rights NGOs: Role Structure and Legal Status, K.U. Leuven, Institute for International Law Working Paper No 14, 21 November 2001,p.7.

76 *Martens*, Examining the (Non-) Status of NGOs in International Law, Indiana Journal of Global Legal Studies, Vol. 10, Issue 2, Article 1, pp. 19 ff.

77 Ibid, p. 21.

78 Ibid.

79 Ibid.

80 Ibid.

Belgium.[81] Article 8 of the 1919 Belgian Act says that "*International associations with their registered offices abroad which are governed by a foreign law* [...] *may in Belgium,* [...] *exercise the rights accruing from their national status. It is not essential that the administration shall include at least one Belgian member*"[82] and is considered an influential text in NGO Law.[83] In practice, this means, for instance, that American NGOs operating in Belgium, like Human Rights Watch, which is based in New York, are regulated under US law, whereas Amnesty International, based in London, has to meet British standards.[84] In one sense, this is a milestone on the path to setting a legal framework regarding NGOs. On the other hand, the deficits of such regulation become apparent. It is still necessary that the particular international NGO is established under the respective national law. Thus, the NGO is first of all dependent on good governance in the NGO legal area of its home state. Furthermore, even when national legislation goes to the extent of acknowledging, within its jurisdiction, the accuracy of operations originating outside their borders, it "cannot and will never be able, without the consent of foreign states, to control those same activities beyond the limits of national territory."[85]

With regard to this thesis, the cornerstone of human rights NGOs is their engagement in pushing governments for more and better human rights commitments and thus being considered advocates for change. While states are, as discussed above, the main subjects of international law and decide whether to agree to (human rights) treaties, pledge benefits or threaten sanctions regarding others human rights behaviour, NGOs are unable to deploy such tools.[86] Instead, NGOs mainly

81 *Martens*, Examining the (Non-) Status of NGOs in International Law, Indiana Journal of Global Legal Studies, Vol. 10, Issue 2, Article 1, pp. 21.

82 Law of 25th October 1919 on International Associations with Scientific Objectives, Article 8, https://uia.org/belgianlaw.

83 *Martens*, Examining the (Non-) Status of NGOs in International Law, Indiana Journal of Global Legal Studies, Vol. 10, Issue 2, Article 1, p.22.

84 Ibid.

85 *Merle*, International Non-governmental Organizations and their Legal Status, Appendix 3.5 of the International Associations Statutes Series vol 1, UIA eds, 1988, https://uia.org/archive/legal-status-3-5.

86 *Hicks*, Human Rights Diplomacy: The NGO Role, in: *O'Flaherty, et al.* (eds.), Human Rights Diplomacy: Contemporary Perspectives, p. 218.

rely (to different degrees) on four elements to be heard: information; expertise; media; and public support.[87] NGOs thereby became shapers of the debate, partners in policy making and overseers of human rights.[88] They are active in almost every field of international human rights practice, advocate for human rights norms and contribute to the drafting of multilateral treaties and resolutions containing such standards.[89]

Whilst the legal position of human rights NGOs under international law is a subject of significant debate, their impact and importance in shaping IHRL, protecting, defending human rights and combating adversaries of human rights is unambiguous. In the international context, headway regarding the legal identity of NGOs has only been made on a regional level. Within Europe, the European Convention on the Recognition of the Legal Personality of International Non-Governmental Organisations can be considered an example of such progress.

### 2.2.2 Legal Status of Non-Governmental Organizations in Europe

As indicated above, in Europe, especially within the European Union, NGOs have a prominent role regarding the shape of human rights policies and the scope within which they operate. The European Convention on the Recognition of the Legal Personality of International Non-Governmental Organisations (hereinafter Convention No. 124), which was adopted in 1986 and entered into force in 1991, contains a general acceptance of the legal identity of an NGO.[90] Today, twelve states are party to the convention[91] whereby it has been, in addition to those countries, expanded to Guernsey, Jersey, and the Isle of Man by the UK.

---

87 *Hicks*, Human Rights Diplomacy: The NGO Role, in: *O'Flaherty, et al.* (eds.), Human Rights Diplomacy: Contemporary Perspectives, p. 218.

88 Ibid, p. 217.

89 *Weissbrodt*, Roles and Responsibilities of Non-State Actors, in: *Shelton* (ed.), The Oxford Handbook of International Human Rights Law, p.721.

90 *Martens*, Examining the (Non-) Status of NGOs in International Law, Indiana Journal of Global Legal Studies, Vol. 10, Issue 2, Article 1, p. 22.

91 State parties are: Austria, Belgium, Cyprus, France, Greece, Liechtenstein, Netherlands, Portugal, Slovenia, Switzerland, The former Yugoslav Republic of Macedonia and the United Kingdom, status of ratification as of 17 October 2018, https://www.

Convention No. 124 sets out in its Article 1 some preconditions which must be fulfilled to recognize the "legal personality of these organisations in order to facilitate their activities at European level"[92]. According to Article 1 of Convention No. 124, an NGO must

> "*(a) have a non-profit-making aim of international utility; (b) have been established by an instrument governed by the internal law of a Party; (c) carry on their activities with effect in at least two States; and (d) have their statutory office in the territory of a Party and the central management and control in the territory of that Party or of another Party.*"[93]

However, not only is the rate of ratification rather low, Article 2 Paragraph 1 simply follows the already examined Belgium Law from 1919 and links the recognition of their legal personality and capacity to the domestic law of the respective member state where the NGO's statutory office is located. Nevertheless, it is the only (for its state parties) legally binding instrument in that regard and can be seen as a recommencement for further debates about the status of NGOs within the CoE. In 1998, these discussions led to the adoption of the Guidelines for the Development and Reinforcement on Non-Governmental Organisations in Europe, followed by the Fundamental Principles on the Status of Non-Governmental Organisations in Europe in 2002.[94] While these documents are not legally binding, the CoE's Committee of Ministers recognised them with contentment, circulated them among its members and created the Group of Specialists on the Legal Status of Non-Governmental Organisations (CJ-S-ONG) in 2005.[95] The expert group was equipped with a mandate on behalf of the European Committee on Legal Co-operation (CDCJ) and entrusted with the task of drafting a recommendation for a legally binding treaty on the legal position of NGOs in Europe, to reflect the already high standing and acknowledged importance of NGOs with regard to human

---

coe.int/en/web/conventions/full-list/-/conventions/treaty/124/signatures?p_auth=QFeq77Fy.

92 European Convention on the Recognition of the Legal Personality of International Non-Governmental Organisations, ETS No 124, 24.IV.1986, Preamble.

93 Ibid, Article 1.

94 Council of Europe, Legal status of non-governmental organisations in Europe Recommendation CM/Rec(2007)14 and explanatory memorandum, 10 October 2007, p. 17.

95 Ibid.

rights policies in Europe.[96] This led to the text of Recommendation CM/Rec(2007)14 presented by the CDCJ on 01 March 2007 and adopted by the Committee of Ministers on 10 October 2007.[97]

Thus, the CoE's decision-making body, the Committee of Ministers, whose task and function is defined under Chapter IV of the Statute of the Council of Europe, has made in accordance with Article 15 lit. b of the Statute the termed Recommendation CM/Rec(2007)14, in which it comprehensively describes its view on the legal position of NGOs in Europe. In this document, the Committee of Ministers strongly acknowledges the important contributions made by NGOs in the field of human rights and democracy and their role as a driving force for the "achievement of the aims and principles of the United Nations Charter and of the Statute of the Council of Europe"[98]. The different methods and the diverse body of activities through which NGOs contribute to improvements in that regard are also noted. Especially worthy of mention here are "the advocacy of changes in law and public policy [...] [and] the monitoring of compliance with existing obligations under national and international law"[99].

The Committee of Ministers notes that NGOs can be established by natural or legal persons or groups and that they are voluntary, self-governing in nature, and with no intention of profit making.[100] Political parties are excluded and they shall not be subject to directions by government bodies.[101] They can have legal personality or not, and be national or international and have the same rights as other – depending on their determined structure – legal or individual entities.[102] The legal environment in which they operate should be benevolent and the relevant rules for obtaining legal personality widely publicized and easily understandable.[103] The ability to effectively participate during public

96 Council of Europe, Legal status of non-governmental organisations in Europe Recommendation CM/Rec(2007)14 and explanatory memorandum, 10 October 2007, p. 17.
97 Ibid.
98 Ibid, p. 5.
99 Ibid.
100 Ibid, p. 7.
101 Ibid.
102 Ibid.
103 Ibid, pp. 10 f.

policy decisions should be secured without discrimination.[104] Foreign NGOs should be treated without prejudice and the same standards applied for their establishment.[105] Only in the case of serious misconduct, bankruptcy or constant inaction can approval be denied.[106] These framework conditions are, however, not newly established through new legislation. Rather, such regulations derive from already existing international treaties, laws and other agreements. The right to establish and operate NGOs at the regional European level is guaranteed by Article 11 of the ECHR and for certain groups or organizational structures by Article 5 of the amended European Social Charter, Articles 3, 7 and 8 of the Framework Convention for the Protection of National Minorities (ETS No. 157), and Article 3 of the Convention on the Participation of Foreigners in Public Life at Local Level (ETS No. 144).[107] Moreover, the host country's compliance with domestic fundamental rights and freedoms legislation and the observance of the basic principles of democracy, including an active contribution to public life and the expression of various and pluralistic views – the main business of NGOs – are the principal characteristics of a successful democracy.

In sum, although there is, in Convention No. 124, a legally binding instrument with regard to the juridical status of NGOs in Europe, it has certain deficits in terms of the number of ratifications, and did not succeed in going beyond the pre-existing ideas of the 1919 Belgium Law to create a new legal concept granting NGOs a legal status detached from the domestic law of their headquarters. Recommendation CM/Rec(2007)14 highlights the remarkable position of NGOs in Europe and underpins the acceptance of this by the CoE's member states, but it also only summarizes existing fundamental rights provisions within the regional framework. However, the position in which NGOs find themselves should not be seen as weak, rather the opposite is true; their right to exist, and to work freely and independently without state intervention and control is established in already accepted and adop-

104 Council of Europe, Legal status of non-governmental organisations in Europe Recommendation CM/Rec(2007)14 and explanatory memorandum, 10 October 2007, p. 16.

105 Ibid, p. 12.

106 Ibid.

107 Ibid, p. 19.

ted human rights conventions which cannot be undercut by the Council's member states. The strength of these systematic approaches should not be underestimated.

## 2.3 Definition of Human Rights Defenders

By now, it has become apparent that it is of crucial importance to define at least the main actors with regard to human rights protection originating from non-state actors, namely civil society and NGOs. This inevitably leads to HRDs, for whom it is also necessary to have an internationally agreed-upon definition.

The United Nations HRD Declaration is a significant starting point in this matter. However, the term human rights defender itself is absent from the declaration on human rights defenders and neither is it mentioned in a defining manner in other legally binding declarations. So, no strict definition exists. The Declaration states in Article 1: "Everyone has the right, individually and in association with others, to promote and to strive for the protection and realization of human rights and fundamental freedoms at the national and international levels"[108]. Other instruments like the EU Guidelines on Human Rights Defenders or the OSCE Guidelines on the Protection of Human Rights Defenders mostly refer to Article 1 of the declaration.[109] Further, there is no standardized procedure to specify a HRD's status.[110] The breadth of the Declaration and other documents referring to it, leave open considerable room for interpretation. Often, people who could arguably be considered HRDs do not define themselves as such. Even more troubling, are situations where states exploit this lack of precision and do not ac-

108 A/RES/53/144, Declaration on the Right and Responsibility of Individuals, Groups and Organs of Society to Promote and Protect Universally Recognized Human Rights and Fundamental Freedoms, 8 March 1999, p. 3, Article 1.

109 Cf. European Union, Ensuring Protection – European Union Guidelines on Human Rights Defenders, 14 June 2004, 10056/1/04, p. 3; OSCE, Guidelines on the Protection of Human Rights Defenders, p. 1.

110 *Nah, et al.*, A Research Agenda for the Protection of Human Rights Defenders, Journal of Human Rights Practice, Volume 5, Issue 3, p. 403.

knowledge people as HRDs or worse, declare them to be perpetrators or terrorists.

Despite the fact that the term HRD is not specifically alluded to in the Declaration, Article 1 gives some guidance on how to define a HRD. Specifically, it is necessary to act in a way which promotes, realizes and defends Human Rights. So, any individual, group or entity can become an HRD as long as they act in the outlined manner. This interpretation follows the United Nations Fact Sheet No. 29 where it is stated that the term HRD:

> "*describe*[s] *people who, individually or with others, act to promote or protect human rights. Human rights defenders are identified above all by what they do and it is through a description of their actions* [...] *and of some of the contexts in which they work* [...] *that the term can best be explained.*"[111]

Thus, it appears that a strong indicator of who is an HRD can be identified by their concrete actions. These actions must, though, be committed within the scope of human rights, accept their universality and be non-violent and peaceful.[112] However, some authors are critical of the UN Fact Sheet's interpretation and argue that in addition to the three main requirements, an ethical vision is necessary to specify a human rights defender.[113] HRDs are simultaneously influenced by their (political and economic) environment and are therefore on one hand agents of social change, affecting their specific realities, and on the other hand are affected by the same specific factors.[114] They are "agents who evolve over time as their awareness of being a defender grows and they establish relationships with other actors in the context of their work."[115] While such realities and contexts are not only influenced by HRDs, but may also transform people into human rights defenders, the term defines a "person based on their activity, work, and action, re-

111 UN Office of the High Commissioner for Human Rights (OHCHR), Fact Sheet No. 29, Human Rights Defenders: Protecting the Right to Defend Human Rights, April 2004, p. 2.

112 *Terto Neto*, Protecting Human Rights Defenders in Latin America, p. 31.

113 Ibid.

114 Ibid.

115 *Fernández / Patel*, Towards developing a critical and ethical approach for better recognising and protecting human rights defenders, The International Journal of Human Rights, Vol. 19 No. 7, p. 904.

gardless of whether the person defines himself or herself as such."[116] This can include "*lawyers, journalists, activists, trade unionists, members of community-based organisations, people in social movements and staff of human rights organisations involved in different work in very different contexts* [...] *including protesters, teachers, students, social workers, health care professionals, community workers, sexual minorities, religious minorities and peace builders, amongst others.*"[117] Besides these definition attempts by researchers, global and regional human rights NGOs have also contributed interpretative suggestions in that regard, most of which tend towards the same direction of discussion.[118] What most approaches have in common is that the main focus lies on the *actions* committed by a person, group or entity. Defining HRDs through their practice might help to overcome the discussion of inclusion and exclusion of certain people by a definition, moving the focus onto what an HRD may or may not have done in a specific context[119] to make a stand for human rights. While there are some concerns about a definition focusing mainly on the actors' actions[120], this inclusive definition is well-suited for a legal evaluation of the international protection framework.

With this in mind, for the purpose of this thesis the term human rights defender describes a person, group or entity acting non-violently to promote, realize and/or defend recognized human rights. This includes the necessary breadth in the definition to cover everything concerned, but is narrow enough to put the focus on the international legal framework, leaving out (also important) purely sociological, ethical or political limitations or requirements.

This discussion about definition approaches and the findings – that the specific context in which someone acts is decisive – clearly elucidates

116 *Terto Neto*, Protecting Human Rights Defenders in Latin America, p.31.

117 *Bennett, et al.*, Critical perspectives on the security and protection of human rights defenders, The International Journal of Human Rights, Volume 19 No. 7,p. 888.

118 Cf. *Fernández / Patel*, Towards developing a critical and ethical approach for better recognising and protecting human rights defenders, The International Journal of Human Rights, Vol. 19 No. 7, pp. 896 ff.

119 Ibid, p. 898.

120 Ibid, p 897.

the vital importance of the space in which civil society and HRDs can engage with one another and (inter)national institutions. Thus, the phenomenon of shrinking or even closing space has significant implications in the context of international human rights law.

# 3 Identification of the Existing Legal Framework to Protect Human Rights Defenders

Although it has been shown difficult to define civil society, non-governmental organizations and human rights defenders acting within the civic space, regulations exist to protect human rights defenders and secure particular civic spaces, granting them a certain leeway in their work. As Margaret Sekaggya, the former UN Special Rapporteur on the situation of human rights defenders instructively observed in her report to the twenty-fifth session of the Human Rights Council in 2014, a reasonable and effective legal environment constitutes one of the best protection mechanisms for HRDs.[121] She argued that:

> *"One of the key elements of a safe and enabling environment for defenders is the existence of laws and provisions [...]that protect, support and empower defenders [...] The adoption of laws that explicitly guarantee the rights contained in the Declaration on Human Rights Defenders is crucial in that it could contribute to building an enabling environment and give these rights legitimacy."*[122]

In light of this, it is necessary to examine firstly the international legal framework and subsequently, with a view to the scope of this thesis, the regional legal framework, namely the European one.

## 3.1 International Legal Framework

With regard to the international sphere, the most universal text is the aforementioned Declaration on the Right and Responsibility of Individuals, Groups and Organs of Society to Promote and Protect Universally Recognized Human Rights and Fundamental Freedoms (HRD

121 A/HRC/25/55, Report of the Special Rapporteur on the Situation of Human Rights Defenders, paras. 62 f.

122 Ibid.

Declaration). The genesis of this document was preceded by long, intense and difficult negotiations. The drafting process before the adoption of the declaration in 1998 took over 15 years and was characterized by strain, discrepancies and compromises.[123] However, the outcome document "marked a milestone in the development of a multilevel, multi-actor international protection regime for the rights of human rights defenders."[124] The adoption of the HRD Declaration led to considerably greater awareness regarding HRDs and their situation, broadening recognition of their need for protection. Also notable is the collective effort by human rights NGOs and state delegations to draft such a strong, beneficial and pragmatic document that is not only addressed to HRDs and States but rather to everyone who recognizes a global human rights regime.[125] Despite being adopted unanimously by the United Nations General Assembly (UNGA), which constitutes a very strong commitment by States, the Declaration is not legally binding.[126] It rather summarizes and reaffirms norms laid down in already existing and legally binding instruments such as the International Covenant on Civil and Political Rights (ICCPR).[127] In particular, this includes: freedom of association (Article 22 ICCPR), freedom of expression and opinion (Article 19 ICCPR), freedom of peaceful assembly (Article 21 ICCPR), the right to provide legal assistance (Article 14(3) ICCPR) and the right to obtain access to information (Article 19 ICCPR).[128] Despite its non-binding character, the HRD Declaration thus helps to explain issues that need clarification, adds to established

---

123 *Bennett, et al.*, Critical perspectives on the security and protection of human rights defenders, The International Journal of Human Rights, Volume 19 No. 7, p. 883.

124 Ibid.

125 UN Office of the High Commissioner for Human Rights (OHCHR), Fact Sheet No. 29, Human Rights Defenders: Protecting the Right to Defend Human Rights, April 2004, p. 19.

126 Ibid.

127 *Eaton*, Human Rights Defenders in the United Nations Framework, 25 Hum. Rts. Defender 5, p. 6.

128 UN Special Rapporteur on the Situation of Human Rights, Commentary to the Declaration on human rights defenders, p. 5.

principles and guides States in protecting those acting as guardians of human rights.[129]

The HRD Declaration with its 20 Articles can be divided into: (a) rights and protection accorded to HRDs, (b) States obligations, (c) accountabilities of everyone and (d) the role of domestic law. Articles 1, 5, 6, 7, 8, 9, 11, 12 and 13 refer to the first part of the provisions (a).[130] The rights listed there include *inter alia*: the conduction of human rights work individually and in association with others; the right to attend public hearings, proceedings and trials in order to determine their compliance with national law and international human rights obligations and to attempt to protect and ensure human rights at domestic and/or international level.[131] Part (b) consists of Articles 2, 9, 12, 14 and 15 and indicates that States also have duties and responsibilities, for instance: the protection, promotion and implementation of all human rights, ensuring that everyone under their jurisdiction is able to benefit from them, the adoption of a legislation which establishes a safe and secure legal environment for HRDs, providing access to remedies and prompt and impartial investigations of alleged human rights violations and the creation of national human rights institutions.[132] Responsibilities of everyone (c) are noted in Articles 10, 11 and 18 and specify the duty to safeguard democracy including its institutions, the promotion of human rights and to respect the rights of others.[133] In part (d) Articles 3 and 4 regulate the connection between the Declaration and domestic and international law in order to apply the highest possible standard of human rights protection.[134]

The protection regime established with the HRD Declaration can be described as composed of five key features. Firstly, the norms and principles laid down deduce, as mentioned, from the already established

129 Lawyers of the Committee for Human Rights, Protecting Human Rights Defenders Analysis of the newly adopted Declaration on Human Rights Defenders, The International Journal of Not-for-Profit Law, Volume 1, Issue 3, March 1999.

130 UN Office of the High Commissioner for Human Rights (OHCHR), Fact Sheet No. 29, Human Rights Defenders: Protecting the Right to Defend Human Rights, April 2004, p. 20.

131 Ibid, p. 21.

132 Ibid.

133 Ibid, p. 22.

134 Ibid.

international human rights system.[135] Over time, policies such as the significance of protecting and promoting 'civil society space'[136] occurred in the system's procedure.[137] Secondly, the regime is goal driven, aiming to protect HRDs in specific contexts and situations which include, for instance, surveillance, torture or arbitrary detention, and which can be inflicted by government officials, corporations or criminal organizations among many others.[138] Thirdly, individuals, groups and communities are the primary subject of protection, elaborating what has been described as a 'human security paradigm'.[139] A holistic and multidimensional perception of human security is recommended and should be divided in three interconnected domains, namely "physical security, digital security and self-care."[140] Fourth, the system is a multi-level regime incorporating all levels, the domestic, regional and international.[141] Lastly, the regime, through its multi-stakeholder approach, involves many actors, ranging from individual defenders, civil society groups, NGOs, national human rights institutions to international institutions and multilateral bodies.[142] All of these establish various tools and tactics to contribute to the protection and encouragement of HRDs. In this light, it is highly advisable for States to make the Declaration a legally binding instrument domestically in order to "facilitate its application by the judiciary and respect for it by State authorities."[143]

135 *Bennett, et al.*, Critical perspectives on the security and protection of human rights defenders, The International Journal of Human Rights, Volume 19 No. 7, p. 884.
136 A/HRC/RES/27/31, 3 October 2014,UN General Assembly Human Rights Council, Civil Society Space; A/HRC/RES/24/21, 9 October 2013, UN General Assembly Human Rights Council, Civil Society Space.
137 *Bennett, et al.*, Critical perspectives on the security and protection of human rights defenders, The International Journal of Human Rights, Volume 19 No. 7, p. 884.
138 Ibid.
139 Ibid.
140 Ibid.
141 Ibid.
142 Ibid.
143 UN Office of the High Commissioner for Human Rights (OHCHR), Fact Sheet No. 29, Human Rights Defenders: Protecting the Right to Defend Human Rights, April 2004, p. 30.

Further, two years after the adoption of the HRD Declaration, the United Nations Commission on Human Rights (predecessor of the UN Human Rights Council) requested in Resolution 2000/61, the UN Secretary General to designate a Special Representative on Human Rights Defenders in order to assist in implementing the Declaration and gathering of information about the global situation of HRDs.[144] According to paragraph 3 of the resolution, the Special Representative's main tasks are:

> "*(a) To seek, receive, examine and respond to information on the situation and the rights of anyone, acting individually or in association with others, to promote and protect human rights and fundamental freedoms; (b) To establish cooperation and conduct dialogue with Governments and other interested actors on the promotion and effective implementation of the Declaration; (c) To recommend effective strategies better to protect human rights defenders and follow up on these recommendations*"[145]

Later the Special Representative became, with renewal of the mandate, the Special Rapporteur on the Situation of Human Rights Defenders. Not only the name changed, but also the tasks of the Special Rapporteur were extended and now contain *inter alia*:

> "*(a) To promote the effective and comprehensive implementation of the Declaration* [...] *Promote and Protect Universally Recognized Human Rights and Fundamental Freedoms through cooperation and constructive dialogue and engagement with Governments, relevant stakeholders and other interested actors; (b) To study, in a comprehensive manner, trends, developments and challenges in relation to the exercise of the right of anyone, acting individually or in association with others* [...] *(e) To integrate a gender perspective* [...] *(f) To work in close coordination with other relevant United Nations bodies, offices, departments and specialized agencies, both at Headquarters and at the country level, and in particular with other special procedures of the Council; (g) To report regularly to the Council and the General Assembly*"[146]

---

144 UN Office of the High Commissioner for Human Rights (OHCHR), Fact Sheet No. 29, Human Rights Defenders: Protecting the Right to Defend Human Rights, April 2004, p. 22.

145 E/CN.4/RES/2000/61, 26 April 2000, UN Commission on Human Rights, Human rights defenders, para. 3.

146 A/HRC/RES/7/8, 27 March 2008, Human Rights Council resolution, Mandate of the Special Rapporteur on the situation of human rights defenders, para. 2.

Other developments regarding the international framework concerning HRDs are, for instance, the Declaration on preventing Sexual Violence in Conflict[147], adopted by the Group of Eight (G8) in 2013 which recognizes the role of women HRDs. The same year, the UNGA adopted the very first resolution on women HRDs.[148] Further, the Human Rights Council adopted various notable resolutions regarding the vital importance of HRDs and their protection. Worth mentioning are Resolution 22/6 of March 2013 on Protecting Human Rights Defenders and Resolution 27/L27/Rev.1 on Human Rights, Sexual Orientation and Gender Identity, wherein States recognized that some HRDs are particularly vulnerable.[149] Moreover the Universal Periodic Review (UPR) is now commonly used to raise concerns about the security and protection of HRDs by various means.[150] The central element with regard to the protection regime is the above-mentioned pressing need to build a 'safe and enabling environment' for HRDs. This means primarily to implement the Declaration into binding legislation to ensure that human rights violations, reprisals and other severe threats against defenders do not remain unpunished.[151] This point will be continuously discussed in this thesis.

## 3.2 Regional Legal Framework

On the regional level, numerous protection mechanisms exist within the various supranational bodies, frequently with varying degrees of protection, implementation and enforcement. How the protective

---

147 G8 Declaration on Preventing Sexual Violence in Conflict, 11 April 2013, https://www.un.org/ruleoflaw/files/G8%20Declaration%20Sexual%20Violence%20in%20Conflict%20-%20April%202013.pdf.

148 A/RES/68/181, 18 December 2013, protecting women human rights defenders.

149 A/HRC/RES/22/6, 12 April 2013, Protecting Human Rights Defenders; A/HRC/27/L.27/Rev.1, 24 September 2014, resolution on Human Rights, Sexual Orientation and Gender Identity.

150 *Bennett, et al.*, Critical perspectives on the security and protection of human rights defenders, The International Journal of Human Rights, Volume 19 No. 7, p. 886.

151 A/69/259, 5 August 2014, Report of the UN Special Rapporteur on the Situation of Human Rights Defenders.

mechanism is designed depends on the peculiarities of each regional system. The following section offers a brief overview on the most important regional legal frameworks, before turning to a more detailed analysis of the European regional system, the focus of this thesis.

### 3.2.1 Africa, Asia, Latin America and the Caribbean

The African Union (AU) as a regional organization, has developed a range of legal provisions in order to protect HRDs. The African Commission on Human Rights adopted in 1999 the Grand Bay Declaration and Plan of Action which clearly notes in paragraph 19 the importance of the protection of HRDs and more importantly, urged African States "to take appropriate steps to implement the Declaration in Africa."[152] In 2003 another declaration, the so-called Kigali Declaration, reiterated the relevance of HRDs, their vulnerability and the value of their involvement in decision-making processes.[153] Later, the African Commission on Human and People's Rights created a Focal Point on Human Rights Defenders in Africa and in 2004, a separate Special Rapporteur for Human Rights Defenders in Africa was established.[154] Worth mentioning is the so-called Kampala Plan of Action (KAPA) which was initiated in 2009 following the Pan-African Conference on Human Rights Defenders in Kampala and which, encouragingly, incorporated not only governments and diplomatic corps, but also local and international NGOs.[155] The KAPA considers as primary goals the improved cooperation among all relevant stakeholders within the region; training and education in the use of the international and regional defence mechanisms; and guidance for states, IGOs, and NGOs to react properly to the necessities of HRDs.[156] This was considered a breakthrough in the region, "since it may lead to the creation of na-

152 Grand Bay Declaration and Plan of Action, 16 April 1999, para. 19, http://www.achpr.org/instruments/grandbay/.

153 Kigali Declaration of 8 May 2003, para. 28, http://www.achpr.org/instruments/kigali/.

154 Protection International, Legislators and Human Rights Defenders, 2011, p. 4.

155 *Quintana / Fernández*, Protection of human rights defenders: Best practices and lessons learnt, Protection International, 2012, p. 10.

156 Ibid.

tional protection mechanisms and the consolidation and strengthening of regional mechanisms."[157]

Similar developments can be observed in other regional systems like the Organization of American States (OAS) in the Latin American and Caribbean area, where, since 1999, annual resolutions regarding HRDs have been adopted.[158] In the 2001 resolution, the OAS's General Assembly called on the Inter-American Commission on Human Rights (IACHR) to monitor the situation of HRDs, leading to the establishment of the IACHR Human Rights Defenders Unit.[159] The Inter-American Court on Human Rights, as the main judicial body for human rights protection in the region, also dealt with cases regarding the work of HRDs and the violation of their rights.[160] The Inter-American human rights protection regime cannot be outlined without mentioning the Centre for Justice and International Law (CEJIL), an NGO considered to be of vital importance and an effective link between the regional system and national organizations, equipped with capabilities and authority to effectively supplement the function and development of the regional system.[161]

The Asian region has seen the emergence of human rights protection mechanisms in recent years. However, in Asia, human rights protection is generally less legalized[162] through formal supranational institutions and consequently, the encouragement and protection of HRDs is also lagging behind. The main protection mechanisms are highly dependent on the will of national governments, local human rights insti-

157 *Quintana / Fernández*, Protection of human rights defenders: Best practices and lessons learnt, Protection International, 2012, p. 11.

158 Ibid, p. 6.

159 OEA/Ser.PAG/RES. 1818 (XXXI-O/01), 5 June 2001.

160 *Quintana / Fernández*, Protection of human rights defenders: Best practices and lessons learnt, Protection International, 2012, p. 6; See further: The cases of *Heliodoro Portugal vs Panama* or that of *Myrna Mack vs Guatemala,* in both cases the liability of the state was established and they admitted responsibility for the murder of the anthropologist and abduction of the trade unionist.

161 *Quintana / Fernández*, Protection of human rights defenders: Best practices and lessons learnt, Protection International, 2012, p. 9.

162 For the three-level approach of legalization see: *Abbot et al.*, The Concept of Legalization, International Organization, Vol. 54, Issue 3, 2012.

tutions and the domestic regime's structure.[163] Notable in regard of overarching human rights safeguarding are the Asian Human Rights Charter, the Asian Human Rights Commission and the Association of South East Asian States (ASEAN). In 2009 an Intergovernmental Commission on Human Rights was inaugurated by ASEAN to promote the protection of human rights, as well as to intensify the regional cooperation in that regard.[164] However, the outcome of those bodies and instruments is far behind what other international organizations, especially the European system, provide.[165]

Therefore, Europe's legal protection regime concerning HRDs will be further illustrated in the next section. Since a higher standard calls for stricter commitments and obligations, it is worth examining the adequacy of the protection standards and the extent to which states comply with their obligations.

### 3.2.2 European Protection Mechanisms

In the European region, despite a relatively strong legal framework and several protective mechanisms regarding human rights violations, issues continue to emerge with the treatment of human rights defenders. Due to Europe's specific governance structure, there are several bodies and institutions dealing with human rights, which might, as already examined in 2.1.1, lead to overlapping mandates or even competition between them. Nonetheless, the strong support for the human rights protection regime, particularly with regard to HRDs, is a unique characteristic of the European system that should not be underestimated. Both the Council of the European Union and the Organization for Security and Cooperation in Europe have established Guidelines for the protection of HRDs. More importantly, the Council of Europe and its renowned human rights protection body, the European Court of Human Rights provide the backbone to the protective regime.

163 *Quintana / Fernández*, Protection of human rights defenders: Best practices and lessons learnt, Protection International, 2012, p. 12.

164 *Bantekas / Oette*, International Human Rights Law and Practice, p. 290.

165 *Quintana / Fernández*, Protection of human rights defenders: Best practices and lessons learnt, Protection International, 2012, p. 12.

The first two important regional documents to mention regarding the protection of HRDs are the European Union Guidelines on Human Rights Defenders (hereinafter the EU Guidelines) and the OSCE Guidelines on the Protection of Human Rights Defenders. In 2014, during the 10th anniversary of the EU Guidelines, the OSCE initiated comprehensive deliberations with HRDs, NGOs and other experts within its regional sphere of competence to develop the OSCE Guidelines on the Protection of Human Rights Defenders.[166] Those two documents aim to improve the support of HRDs and especially marginalized groups like women human rights defenders or LGBTI activists, focusing on the implementation of existing mechanisms and, in line with the former UN Special Rapporteur's call, the "creation of a safe and enabling environment"[167], for HRDs.[168] In addition to policy objectives and practical initiatives, the Guidelines offer further instruction, for instance for diplomats to act in line with their obligations towards HRDs.[169] Also established through the European Council of the EU, is the Working Party on Human Rights (COHOM) which operates in the sphere of developing human rights policy in the EU's foreign affairs and to achieve better protection for HRDs.[170] While the idea behind COHOM's mandate and the guidelines for diplomats was probably for the protection of HRDs by diplomatic personnel outside of Europe, current developments within Europe make those instruments important for internal affairs as well.

Within this framework, the stated HRD protection guidelines by the EU and the OSCE as well as ECHR itself as efficient instruments to safeguard human rights defenders will be outlined in the following.

166 *Bennett, et al.*, Critical perspectives on the security and protection of human rights defenders, The International Journal of Human Rights, Volume 19 No. 7, p. 885 f.

167 A/HRC/25/55, Report of the Special Rapporteur on the Situation of Human Rights Defenders, paras. 62 f.

168 *Bennett, et al.*, Critical perspectives on the security and protection of human rights defenders, The International Journal of Human Rights, Volume 19 No. 7, p. 885 f.

169 *Bennett*, European Union Guidelines on Human Rights Defenders: a review of policy and practice towards effective implementation, The International Journal of Human Rights, Vol. 19 No. 7, p. 909.

170 Ibid.

#### 3.2.2.1 European Union Guidelines on Human Rights Defenders

In addition to the United Nations HRD protection regime, the European Union adopted its own measures and mechanisms to clarify the status and importance of HRDs and their need to be specifically protected. The European Union Guidelines on Human Rights Defenders were created in 2004 and again revised in 2008 (becoming therefore important as the UN Human Rights Council was only established after the initial guidelines and is now recognized by them)[171]. In accordance with Article 2, 3(5) and 21(2) lit. b of the Treaty of the European Union, the EU Guidelines can be considered an instrument to "consolidate and support democracy, the rule of law, human rights and the principles of international law" (Article 21(2) lit. b TEU). In defining HRDs, the EU Guidelines refer to the United Nations HRD Declaration, citing its Article 1 and subsequently summarizing HRDs as

> "*individuals, groups and organs of society that promote and protect universally recognised human rights and fundamental freedoms* [...] *seek the promotion and protection of civil and political rights as well as the promotion, protection and realisation of economic, social and cultural rights* [...] *promote and protect the rights of members of groups such as indigenous communities.*"[172]

There the EU Guidelines go beyond the UN Declaration, firstly with the explicit mention of the name 'human rights defender', while the UN omitted that term[173] and secondly, by concretizing and adding economic social and cultural rights and including indigenous communities. The exclusion of individuals or groups violently pursuing those goals is even more explicitly incorporated in the EU Guidelines. As a primary goal, the EU Guidelines identify securing a safe and free environment which is the basic prerequisite for an actually available scope of action for HRDs and their work.[174] It behove the aforemen-

171 *Baranowska, et al.*, EU human rights engagement in UN bodies, Deliverable 5.1, 10.7404/FRAME.REPS. 5.1, 2014, p. 175.

172 European Union, Ensuring Protection – European Union Guidelines on Human Rights Defenders, 14 June 2004, 10056/1/04, para. 3.

173 *Baranowska, et al.*, EU human rights engagement in UN bodies, Deliverable 5.1, 10.7404/FRAME.REPS. 5.1, 2014, p. 175.

174 Cf. European Union, Ensuring Protection – European Union Guidelines on Human Rights Defenders, 14 June 2004, 10056/1/04, para. 11.

tioned COHOM to oversee the effective implementation and operationalization of the Guidelines and the recommendations contained therein.[175] The close link between the UN Declaration and the EU Guidelines is evident through the entire EU document and elucidates thereby the high degree of acceptance of the HRD Declaration in Europe, even despite its non-binding nature. The EU Guidelines build on and clarify, to a certain level, the UN Declaration. The Guidelines call, for instance, on States to judge even fierce criticism of their government's leadership or actions not as something negative or threatening, since leaving space for free and independent thought and speech, including criticism is required to respect fundamental human rights and is central to democracy.[176] Rather, governments should cooperate with HRDs and engage them in drafting appropriate legislations or national strategies regarding human rights policies.[177] The above, better analysed in 2.3, explains the importance of defining the form of 'actions' an HRD might undertake, and it is also identified by the EU Guidelines, namely "*documenting violations; seeking remedies for victims of such violations through the provision of legal, psychological, medical or other support; and combating cultures of impunity which serve to cloak systematic and repeated breaches of human rights and fundamental freedoms.*"[178]

As noted, the EU Guidelines are, in typical fashion for such instruments, not legally binding. However, they can be viewed as a source of "additional structure, a sense of purpose, coherence and legitimacy to the actions undertaken before."[179] Thus the Guidelines rely on the established regional and international legal framework and also on rec-

175 European Union, Ensuring Protection – European Union Guidelines on Human Rights Defenders, 14 June 2004, 10056/1/04, para. 14; *Bennett*, A Protection Regime in Need of Committed Action: European Union Support for Human Rights Defenders, in: *Isa Gómez, et al.*, EU Human Rights and Democratization Policies: Achievements and Challenges, p.146.

176 European Union, Ensuring Protection – European Union Guidelines on Human Rights Defenders, 14 June 2004, 10056/1/04, para. 5.

177 Ibid.

178 Ibid, para. 4.

179 Thematic evaluation of the European Commission support to respect of Human Rights and Fundamental Freedoms, Consortium PARTICIP-ADE–DIE–DRN-ECDPM-ODI, Final Report Vol. 1, p. 51.

ognized policy instruments to substantiate their acceptance.[180] The legally binding protections upon which the Guidelines are based are apparently the same as in the UN Declaration (e.g. the ICCPR), but naturally correspond to their counterparts articulated in the European Convention on Human Rights, including Articles 9, 10 or 11 ECHR among others. Thus, the EU Guidelines are not meant to export or impose European values on other countries, but through the incorporation of international norms, they contribute to the universal human rights regime. International human rights laws provide the normative ground for them and hence increase their legitimacy.[181]

Generally, EU guidelines aim to achieve the EU's overall Common Foreign and Security Policy. Two sets of EU guidelines, namely those on HRDs and on torture, lay out operational elements that provide the means which member states can efficaciously accomplish the stated objectives.[182] That the Guidelines refer mainly in its wording to non-EU countries or so called third countries (for instance in paragraph 1, 7 or 11 among others) has not been neglected. Among those states are however countries that are not EU members but members of the CoE and thus, states relevant to this thesis. Moreover, it is arguable that the EU has the duty to follow its foreign policy norms even more stringently in its internal matters. Complementing this view, the CoE's Parliamentary Assembly has adopted several resolutions and recommendations referring to the need to protect HRDs within the Council's member states. What most of those recommendations and resolutions have in common is that they call on States as "first and foremost"[183] responsible for the protection of HRDs, which consequently implies the need to provide a safe and enabling environment for them. Substantively, this entails implementing the UN Declaration and/or the EU Guidelines into domestic law. Worth mentioning in this regard are Resolution 1891 from 2012 in which the Parliamentary Assembly urged States to pay tribute to HRDs and also insistently excoriates all

180 *Wouters / Hermez*, EU Guidelines on Human Rights as a Foreign Policy Instrument: An Assessment, 2016, p. 13.

181 Ibid, p. 14.

182 Ibid, p. 6.

183 PACE Resolution 2095 (2016), para. 3,PACE Resolution 1891 (2012), para. 4.

attacks against HRDs.[184] Resolution 2095 from 2016 references the legal status of NGOs[185] and Resolution 1660[186] of 2009 as well as Recommendation 2085, issued in 2006,[187] both explicitly refer to the OSCE and its established improvements regarding the protection of HRDs. In this connection, the OSCE Guidelines on the Protection of Human Rights Defenders should meaningfully be taken into consideration for a comprehensive picture of the European framework.

#### 3.2.2.2 OSCE Guidelines on the Protection of Human Rights Defenders

The journey towards adopting the OSCE Guidelines on the Protection of Human Rights defenders (hereinafter OSCE Guidelines) began in 1975 with the Helsinki Final Act,[188] continued with the Document of the Copenhagen Meeting of the Conference on the Human Dimension of the CSCE[189] in 1990, passed through the 1994 Budapest Document, where the "need for protection of human rights defenders"[190] was explicitly mentioned, and through other ongoing commitments and outcome documents up to the 2014 OSCE Guidelines.[191] The aforementioned earlier OSCE documents have not used the name "HRD," but have implicitly recognized the crucial role that the civil society and HRDs have in fulfilling collective objectives within the OSCE.[192] The decisive push to develop the OSCE Guidelines came from a network of CSOs on the brink of the OSCE Ministerial Council in Dublin in 2012.[193] They made a joint statement[194] raising concerns about the

---

184 PACE Resolution 1891 (2012), paras. 1 and 3.

185 PACE Resolution 2095 (2016), para. 1.

186 PACE Resolution 1660 (2009).

187 PACE Recommendation 2085 (2016).

188 Conference on Security and Co-Operation in Europe Final Act (Helsinki Final Act), 1975, https://www.osce.org/helsinki-final-act?download=true.

189 Document of the Copenhagen Meeting of the Conference on the Human Dimension of the CSCE, https://www.osce.org/odihr/19394?download=true.

190 CSCE Budapest Document 1994, Towards a Genuine Partnership in a New Era, para. 18, https://www.osce.org/mc/39554?download=true.

191 OSCE, Guidelines on the Protection of Human Rights Defenders, p. ix.

192 Ibid.

193 Ibid.

194 Dublin Declaration – Security of human rights defenders: time for OSCE to act, Dublin, 5 December 2012, http://www.civicsolidarity.org/ sites/default/files/dublin_declaration_on_human_rights_defenders_final.pdf.

threats HRDs were facing, which led the OSCE Office for Democratic Institutions and Human Rights (ODIHR) to begin developing the guidelines.[195]

It is worth mentioning that the OSCE did not only cover the European region but also Central Asian and North American countries, 57 in total. This expands the regional protection regime and affirms the commitment of the OSCE member States to adhere to those principles. The OSCE as – in accordance with Chapter VIII of the United Nations Charter, – a 'regional arrangement' has, despite its observer status in the GA, no legal international personality.[196] The OSCE Guidelines' aim, though, is not to create new norms or special rights for HRDs, but rather, as the aforementioned instruments – the UN Declaration and EU Guidelines – to elaborate already generally accepted human rights norms.[197] Thus, the Guidelines are directed to contribute to the protective regime and set its particularly practical focus on the "protection of the human rights of those who are at risk as a result of their human rights work."[198]

With regard to the definition of the term "human rights defender", the OSCE Guidelines refer to Article 1 of the United Nations HRD Declaration, explicitly adding (like the EU Guidelines) the non-violent or peaceful condition.[199] Remarkable in the OSCE Guidelines is, then, Paragraph 1, as it clarifies that the right to defend human rights is itself a generally recognized fundamental right.[200] It is substantiated from "universal human rights, which are indivisible, interdependent and interrelated, and which OSCE participating States have committed to respect, protect and fulfil for everyone on their territory and subject to their jurisdiction."[201] The subsequent paragraphs also highlight the essential role of HRDs in a democratic society and their need for protection. That States inherently have the primary responsibility to protect HRDs is also separately emphasized with a list of positive and negative

195 OSCE, Guidelines on the Protection of Human Rights Defenders, p. ix.
196 *Von Arnauld*, Völkerrecht, p. 73, para. 176.
197 OSCE, Guidelines on the Protection of Human Rights Defenders, p. xi.
198 Ibid.
199 Ibid, p.1.
200 Ibid, p. 1, p. 23.
201 Ibid, p. 1.

obligations countries have under international law. The OSCE Guidelines thus reaffirm the requirement that states provide a safe and enabling environment, as demanded by many stakeholders. This holds especially true for the legal, administrative and institutional framework. Furthermore, it is precisely outlined that non-state actors are also accountable regarding the realization of human rights. It is further emphasized that restrictions or limitations on human rights might be possible but only under restricted conditions[202]

The greatest difference between the UN Declaration and the EU Guidelines on one side and the OSCE Guidelines on the other, and the reason for which it is crucial to analyse the OSCE Guidelines separately, is the mere extent of the latter document. While the EU and UN documents can mainly be seen as a declaration of intent in summarizing and compiling the international norms which cater to HRDs, the OSCE Guidelines are much more detailed and might be seen as kind of a commentary to the other documents. For instance, In the OSCE Guidelines, it is not only stated that States have the obligation to protect HRDs, it is rather explained where the substance of this obligation is grounded in international law.[203] Moreover the threats HRDs are facing are not merely illustrated abstractly, the concrete risks, including enforced disappearances, use of force, ill-treatment or even only verbal abuse and many others, are directly acknowledged.[204]

To give but one example regarding this detailed differentiation, the right to private life in the OSCE Guidelines is listed under Section A, the "General Principles underpinning the protection of human rights defenders", where it is observed that this right belongs to the area of granting a safe and enabling environment by the State,[205] itemizing in detail the States' obligation to

> "*refrain from any unlawful or arbitrary interference with the privacy,* [...] *of human rights defenders,* [...] *and to protect them from such interference*

202 OSCE, Guidelines on the Protection of Human Rights Defenders, p. 3, para 11, pp. 39 ff., paras 51–62.

203 See for instance States obligations and where they occur pp. 28 ff., paras 18–25 OSCE, Guidelines on the Protection of Human Rights Defenders.

204 Cf. OSCE, Guidelines on the Protection of Human Rights Defenders, p. 45, para 66.

205 Ibid, p. 2, para 6.

> *by others through legislative and other measures.*[…] [and] *acknowledge that human rights defenders have a special need for protection from undue interference in their private life due to the nature of their work.*"[206]

And finally, under Section B, the 'Explanatory Report' component, it is described where those duties are rooted in international law; namely in Article 17 ICCPR, Article 8 ECHR and Article 11 of the American Convention on Human Rights (ACHR) and beyond that, court decisions, general comments or resolutions by international bodies and Special Rapporteur reports relevant to the specific rights matters.[207]

Notably, this detailed itemization closes the gap between the very broad and abstract principles laid down in the UN Declaration and EU Guidelines. It curtails the scope of interpretation and thus also reduces the risk for unjustified explanations by human rights violators. However, it is arguable that this could also narrow the scope of application and maybe impose the risk of leaving violations or vulnerable people out. To this it can be countered that the OSCE Guidelines are at first not legally binding and further they do not contain any exhaustive list neither of violations, nor of protective obligations or other. Hence, they do not diminish the scope of application.

In sum, it can be stated that the OSCE Guidelines are guidelines within the meaning of actual guiding principles. They not only call on actors to accept the universally agreed upon human rights norms, they explain how they occur and give practical guidance for all respective stakeholders, suggesting which actions and omissions to take.

#### 3.2.2.3 Protection Under the European Convention on Human Rights

In the European Union, the main instrument for the protection of human rights and thus for HRDs and the civil society is indubitably the European Convention on Human Rights. The Convention was adopted in 1950 and has contributed to a common perception of human rights protection by taking "the first steps for the collective enforcement of certain of the Rights stated in the Universal Declaration".[208] This ap-

206 OSCE, Guidelines on the Protection of Human Rights Defenders, p. 17 ff., paras 85–89.

207 Ibid, p. 111 ff., paras 241–258.

208 European Convention on Human Rights, Preamble.

proach can be considered as a response to the predictably insufficient capacity to achieve consensus for implementing the UDHR within the UN, due to the debilitating effect of the Cold War.[209] This can, in passing, be seen as virtue of having diverse systems – the international level stagnates, while the regional is taking the helm.[210] Initially, the ECHR implemented two monitoring institutions: a European Court of Human Rights and a European Commission on Human Rights.[211] While jurisdiction and the individual complaint procedure were restricted at the beginning, it was nonetheless the first international body providing legal redress for those who, under the recognized Convention, had suffered violations of their fundamental rights by a state party.[212] It is notable that the individual became subject of international law, able to both file an appeal against a State and, ultimately, get a binding decision by an international court.[213] Later, the European system developed continuously, strengthening its institutions and especially improving the complaint procedure. This led to Protocol No. 11 to the European Convention on Human Rights in 1998,[214] which abrogated the European Commission and instituted a now full-time Court.[215] The new European Court of Human Rights (hereinafter ECtHR) was equipped with obligatory jurisdiction over all State parties to the Convention and individuals could now directly access the Court.[216]

This development is necessary to highlight, bearing in mind this thesis' purpose, since the individual complaint mechanism is significant for the protection of HRDs and further clarifies the role of NGOs within the legal regime. The vital importance of the civil society becomes clear, whereby it should be noted that the degree of effective provision

209 *Heyns / Killander*, Universality and the Growth of Regional Systems, in: in: *Shelton* (ed.), The Oxford Handbook of International Human Rights Law, p. 675.

210 Ibid, p. 676.

211 Ibid.

212 Ibid.

213 Ibid.

214 Protocol No. 11 to the Convention for the Protection of Human Rights and Fundamental Freedoms, restructuring the control machinery established thereby, ETS No.155.

215 *Heyns / Killander*, Universality and the Growth of Regional Systems, in: in: *Shelton* (ed.), The Oxford Handbook of International Human Rights Law, p. 676.

216 Ibid.

of fundamental rights and freedoms, quasi the existence of a safe and enabling environment, determined the extent to what a civil society, its function and potential is enshrined.[217] Thus in this context it is necessary to take a closer look on the admissibility criteria to lodge a complaint, particularly on the competence *ratione personae* and the so called 'victim status' (Article 34 ECHR) pertaining to it. Article 34 ECHR states that claims can be brought by "any person, non-governmental organisation or group of individuals." This is an indication of the Court's success and outstanding position in human rights protection, described by some authors as the greatest achievement of the Convention's drafters.[218] Or as Janis et al state, the ECHR "establishes not only the world's most successful system of international law for the protection of human rights, but one of the most advanced forms of any kind of international legal process."[219]

However, it cannot be denied that this opening towards a more accessible individual protection regime also caused some difficulties. The number of cases the Court had to deal with increased rapidly because of the possibility for direct individual applications and additionally because of the accession wave of Eastern European countries and Russia in the 1990s.[220] The overwhelming caseload prompted the CoE in 2004 to bring forward another Protocol (Protocol No. 14) to enhance the Court's functionality. However, Russia did not ratify Protocol 14 until 2010, which forced the CoE to produce Protocol 14bis to implement the reforms even without Russia's ratification. Regardless, it became evident at the beginning of the drafting process that the novelties would not have been sufficient to offset the difficulties brought on by the immense caseload.[221] Fortunately, the situation improved and by the end of 2012, the Court announced that, for the first time since 1998, pending applications decreased, the number of decisions in-

217 *Van Veen*, Civil Society in Europe and the European Convention on Human Rights, in: *Van der Ploeg / Van Veen / Versteegh* (eds.), Civil Society in Europe: Minimum Norms and Optimum Conditions of its Regulation, p. 8.

218 *Hodson*, NGOs and the Struggle for Human Rights in Europe, p.18.

219 *Janis, et al.*, European Human Rights Law: Texts and Materials, p.3.

220 *Heyns / Killander*, Universality and the Growth of Regional Systems, in: in: *Shelton* (ed.), The Oxford Handbook of International Human Rights Law, p. 677.

221 *Hodson*, NGOs and the Struggle for Human Rights in Europe, p.19.

creased a trend that appears to be continuing.[222] The main factor has been Protocol 14's reforms to the laborious case-selection procedure, shifting the admissibility process from a Committee (three judges, one judge rapporteur and one Registry lawyer) to a single-judge formation (one judge and one Registry rapporteur), or so called '*juge unique*' (Article 27, 24(2) ECHR).[223] The reason for this is that 90 percent of the submitted applications were inadmissible.[224] A second important development is that the Committee of Ministers, as executive organ of the CoE and responsible for the implementation of the judgements, shall now have the authority to launch infringement proceedings when a member state fails to adhere to its commitments.[225] This rests on the high proportion of repetitive cases (55 percent of the ECHR cases) due to non-compliance with the Court's judgements.[226] One last notable reform is the new Article 35(3) lit. b ECHR which states that the Court can declare an application as inadmissible when "the applicant has not suffered a significant disadvantage [...]." This means that the violation must reach a minimum degree of severity in order to be considered admissible by an international court.[227] Protocols No. 15 and No. 16 aim in the same direction and try to reform the Court's procedure, whereas Protocol No. 15 is currently not entered into force.[228]

This excursus is important to trace since the developments regarding individual applications not only challenged the Court, as they also significantly improved the legal protection regime for HRDs and the space for civil society within Europe.

Within the Courts jurisdiction, human rights defenders bear, as individuals, all rights enshrined in the ECHR. Somewhat different is the situation regarding NGOs. It is vitally important that they can bring cases to the ECtHR, in view of the above outlined issue of civil society.

---

222 *De Schutter*, International Human Rights Law: Cases, Materials, Commentary, p. 986.

223 *Zysset*, The ECHR and Human Rights Theory: Reconciling the Moral and the Political Conceptions, p.89.

224 Ibid.

225 Ibid.

226 Ibid.

227 *Jacobs / White / Ovey*, The European Convention on Human Rights, p. 44.

228 Cf. Complete list of the Council of Europe's treaties, Status as of 08 January 2019, https://www.coe.int/en/web/conventions/full-list.

Beyond that, NGOs can only be independent bearers of rights insofar as the rights are applicable to them.[229] Although the ECHR makes reference to 'democratic society'[230] and not 'civil society,' the two concepts are closely intertwined and presuppose each other. Furthermore, since the term 'democratic society' in the ECHR is reserved to possible restrictions on fundamental rights, it becomes even more interesting in conjunction with the concept of 'civil society'. A main characteristic of the ECHR is that many of the basic rights granted to individuals and organisations are not absolute – States may impose restrictions on them. Those limitations must however fulfil certain prerequisites to be permitted and there, the 'necessity test' (a limitation must be necessary in a democratic society) comes into play. This test generally follows a pattern. However, certain circumstances and specific characteristics of the concerned rights and freedoms affect the legality of a giving limitation.[231] A detailed outline of all permissible limitations is likely impossible and certainly beyond the purpose of this thesis. However, in general, the so called 'three-fold' test, established by the Court through its jurisprudence, implies that restrictions can be justifiable if they are (1) prescribed by law, (2) have a legitimate aim and (3) whether the limitation is necessary in a democratic society.[232] The latter is of particular interest for this thesis. The main issues regarding HRDs and their rights engage the freedom of expression and association. In several judgements, the ECtHR considers the extent to which people enjoy these rights to be an indicator of effective social and political participation, and thus constitutive elements of a democratic society.[233] The

229 *Van Veen*, Civil Society in Europe and the European Convention on Human Rights, in: *Van der Ploeg / Van Veen / Versteegh* (eds.), Civil Society in Europe: Minimum Norms and Optimum Conditions of its Regulation, p. 9.

230 Cf. Article 6, 8, 9, 10, 11 ECHR.

231 *Van Veen*, Civil Society in Europe and the European Convention on Human Rights, in: *Van der Ploeg / Van Veen / Versteegh* (eds.), Civil Society in Europe: Minimum Norms and Optimum Conditions of its Regulation, p. 16.

232 *Jacobs / White / Ovey*, The European Convention on Human Rights pp. 343 ff.

233 Cf. *Gorzelik and Others v. Poland* [GC], no. 44158/98, § 88, ECHR 2004-I; *Sidiropoulos and Others v. Greece*, 10 July 1998, § 40, *Reports of Judgments and Decisions* 1998-IV; *United Communist Party of Turkey and Others v. Turkey* [GC], judgment of 30 January 1998, Reports 1998-I, §§ 42 ff.; *Socialist Party and Others v. Turkey*[GC], judgment of 25 May 1998, Reports 1998-III, §§ 41 ff.; *Refah Partisi (the Welfare Party) and Others v. Turkey* [GC] no. 41340/98, 41342/98, 41343/98 et al.

Court therefore examines limitations on these rights very closely. The Court's interpretation of a democratic society, as reflected in its jurisprudence, can be transferred onto the concept of civil society as the freedom of individuals and organisations to partake in social and political sphere is set as a prerequisite.[234]

Another striking point is the role of NGOs under the Convention, on one hand as holders of rights and on the other as litigators before the Court. While the latter will subsequently be discussed, the already mentioned ability of NGOs to hold fundamental rights, guaranteed by an international human rights treaty, is remarkable. While some rights are obviously not applicable to NGOs, like Article 2 ECHR (right to life) or Article 5 ECHR (personal freedom and safety), others, such as freedom of expression (Article 10), freedom of association (Article 11), right to a fair trial (Article 6) or the right to property (Article 1 of Protocol No. 1) can undoubtedly be claimed by them. Consequently, restrictions on those rights, applicable to CSOs and NGOs, can only be made within the normative framework accorded by the Convention. Some examples that illustrate that are, for instance, the case of the Swiss non-governmental organization *GRA Stiftung gegen Rassismus und Antisemitismus v. Switzerland.*[235] In that case, the ECtHR found a violation of Article 10 ECHR by the State for prosecuting the NGO after they had declared a politician's speech as 'verbal racism' in the context of the controversial discussion about a referendum which aimed to ban minarets in Switzerland.[236] The Court found in that case that "Freedom of expression constitutes one of the essential foundations of a democratic society and one of the basic conditions for its progress and for each individual's self-fulfillment"[237] and that the imposed sanctions against the NGO "may have had a 'chilling effect' on the exercise of the applicant organisation's freedom of expression as it may have discouraged it from pursuing its statutory aims and criticis-

234 *Van Veen*, Civil Society in Europe and the European Convention on Human Rights, in: *Van der Ploeg / Van Veen / Versteegh* (eds.), Civil Society in Europe: Minimum Norms and Optimum Conditions of its Regulation, p. 12.

235 *GRA Stiftung gegen Rassismus und Antisemitismus v. Switzerland*, no. 18597/13, judgement of 9 January 2018.

236 Ibid.

237 Ibid, § 51.

ing political statements and policies in the future."[238] Here, the Court affirms the important role of NGOs as public watchdogs in a democracy with a strong civil society.

Furthermore, many applications against Azerbaijan were lodged with regard to the country's restrictive NGO registration laws. The laws made it nearly impossible to officially register as an NGO and gave the Azerbaijani Ministry of Justice excessive authority to intervene in NGOs' internal operations or even to seek court authority to liquidate an NGO although it has not broken any law.[239] The Court found in all of the applications: *Tebieti Mühafize Cemiyyeti and Israfilov v. Azerbaijan; Ramazanova v. Azerbaijan; Ismayilov v. Azerbaijan; Nasibova v. Azerbaijan* and *Aliyev and others v. Azerbaijan, a violation of Article 11 ECHR, the freedom of association.*[240] In those decisions, the Court consistently affirmed that the denial of NGO status reached the level of an "interference with the applicants' exercise of their right to freedom of association."[241] Further, to underline this, the Court found that "*the right to form an association is an inherent part of the right set forth in Article 11. That citizens should be able to form a legal entity* [...] *is one of the most important aspects of the right to freedom of association, without which that right would be deprived of any meaning. The way in which national legislation enshrines this freedom* [...] *reveal the state of democracy in the country concerned.*"[242]

These and the above identified protection mechanism make it clear that the ECHR has explicitly set a legal framework, which not only

238 *GRA Stiftung gegen Rassismus und Antisemitismus v. Switzerland*, no. 18597/13, judgement of 9 January 2018, § 78.

239 *Guluzade / Bourjaily*, The NGO Law: Azerbaijan Loses Another Case in the European Court, The International Journal of Not-for-Profit Law, Volume 12, Issue 3, May 2010.

240 Cf. the cases: *Tebieti Mühafize Cemiyyeti and Israfilov v. Azerbaijan* no. 37083/03, judgement of 8 Ocotber 2009; *Ramazanova and Others v. Azerbaijan* no. 44363/02, judgement of 1 February 2007; *Ismayilov v. Azerbaijan* no. 4439/0, judgement of 17 January 2008; *Nasibova v. Azerbaijan* no. 4307/04, judgement of 18 October 2007; and *Aliyev and others v. Azerbaijan* no. 28736/05, *judgement of 18 December 2008.*

241 *Ramazanova and Others v. Azerbaijan*, no. 44363/02, judgement of 1 February 2007, § 55.

242 Ibid, § 54.

enumerates rights and gives guidance as well as recommendations, but also makes them enforceable before an international court. The acceptance and recognition on both sides, by States and civil society, through both the admissibility criteria (individuals and NGOs) and especially the 'necessary in a democratic society' test, encouraged this.

#### 3.2.2.4 Non-Governmental Organizations as Litigator Before the European Court of Human Rights

The above-mentioned situation of NGOs acting as litigators before the Court is somewhat specific and also controversial. Despite the fact that NGOs are explicitly mentioned in Article 34 ECHR, the 'victim status' was actually construed in such a way that only someone directly affected by a violation could file an application.[243] Hence it would not be possible for an NGO to lodge a complaint on behalf of someone if the NGO was not directly affected by the violation itself. On one side, this admissibility rule would prevent applications attempting to challenge domestic law in the abstract – or so called '*actio popularis*.'[244] Screening out such cases mitigates the risk of the Court being overwhelmed with cases. Moreover, there is, even among Court officials, certain mistrust towards NGOs, seen as pursuing their own agenda instead of representing victims.[245] Furthermore, the Court actually developed case law prohibiting NGOs to lodge complaints when they are not directly affected.[246] This procedure is unfortunately more restrictive than, for instance, the Inter-American Human Rights System, where public interests can be brought up by NGOs.[247]

On the other side, significant developments have been -at least since the case of *Centre for Legal Resources (CLR) on behalf of Valentin Câm-*

243 *Harris / O'Boyle / Warbrick*, Law of the European Convention on Human Rights pp. 84 ff.

244 Ibid, p. 85.

245 *Haddad*, The Hidden Hands of Justice: NGOs, Human Rights and International Courts, p. 61.

246 *Cichowski*, Civil Society and the European Court of Human Rights, in: *Christoffersen / Madsen* (eds.), The European Court of Human Rights between Law and Politics, p. 85.

247 *Haddad*, The Hidden Hands of Justice: NGOs, Human Rights and International Courts, p. 61.

*peanu v. Romania*[248]– made by the Court. The decision was seen as a landmark or even breakthrough with regard to the legal standing of NGOs before the ECtHR.[249] The exceptional issue in this case is that the CLR could lodge the complaint on behalf of Mr Câmpeanu (since at the time of filing, he had already passed away), despite the fact that the NGO was neither directly or indirectly affected by the violation, by saying that "the Court is satisfied that in the exceptional circumstances of this case and bearing in mind the serious nature of the allegations, it should be open to the CLR to act as a representative of Mr Câmpeanu."[250] From there, this kind of exception from the 'victim status' rule can be found in at least two other cases: *Kondrulin v. Russia*[251] and the case of *Association for the Defence of Human Rights in Romania – Helsinki Committee on Behalf of Ionel Garcea v. Romania*[252]. Thus, the involvement of NGOs in ECHR litigation might be considered as going beyond strict *amicus curiae* participation. However, it is still an exception and in all cases one reason – among other decisive ones – for the Court's flexibility was that the victims of the violations were already deceased. Nonetheless, the possibility is now given with regards to people with disabilities (the second decisive reason for letting an NGO lodge the complaint in the mentioned cases), which could be seen by some NGOs as a beneficial and turning point for future applications. However, the risks with granting NGOs such standing should not be left unconsidered. States might react and tighten their laws regarding NGOs and thus making it even more difficult for them to effectively do

248 *Centre for Legal Resources (CLR) on behalf of Valentin Câmpeanu v. Romania* [GC], no. 47848/08, judgement of 17 July 2014.

249 *De Vylder*, Rewriting CLR on behalf of Valentin Campeanu v Romania (ECtHR): actio popularis as ultimum remedium to enhance access to justice of victims with a mental disability, in: *Brems / Desmet* (eds.), Integrated Human Rights in Practice: Rewriting Human Rights Decisions, p. 289 ff.

250 *Centre for Legal Resources (CLR) on behalf of Valentin Câmpeanu v. Romania* [GC], no. 47848/08, judgement of 17 July 2014, § 112.

251 *Kondrulin v. Russia*, no. 12987/15, judgement of 30 January 2017.

252 Association for the Defence of Human Rights in Romania – Helsinki Committee on behalf of Ionel Garcea v. Romania, no. 2959/11, judgement of 24. March 2015, § 45.

their work.[253] This trend is already observable in states turning toward authoritarianism. Moreover, when the Court keeps enforcing that NGOs can only in 'exceptional circumstances' act on behalf of someone, the risk of declaring a claim inadmissible is high and therefore the prospect of success is relatively slight, especially in the case of small and underfunded NGOs.[254] Consequently, as NGOs step back due to insecurities regarding admissibility criteria, vulnerable people would be left behind and their voices unheard. Finally, states would, owing to the lack of binding case law, see no reason to change their practice.[255] A vicious circle would thus be created. Having this in mind, it is remarkable that statistically human rights NGOs came most often into play when applications concerned Articles 2 (right to life) and 3 (prohibition of torture) ECHR and thus the most severe violations, oftentimes committed against the most vulnerable persons.[256] Hence, despite the fact that the 'victim status' clause in some way restricts the leeway of NGOs, they are definitely an undeniably important actors in the European human rights system.

Furthermore, at least since Protocol No. 11 became obligatory in 1998, civil society HRDs and NGOs, became important third-party interveners and thus, the aforementioned *amicus curiae* briefings also became weightier. NGOs are considered by the Court as experts with particular knowledge and capacity to defend vulnerable people with otherwise no representatives.[257] This is reflected in Article 36(2) ECHR where it is stated that the President of the Court can "invite any High Contracting Party which is not a party to the proceedings or any person concerned who is not the applicant to submit written comments or take part in hearings." This of course includes civil society actors like HRDs or NGOs. This practice expands the options for those actors to have an

---

253 *De Vylder*, Rewriting CLR on behalf of Valentin Campeanu v Romania (ECtHR): actio popularis as ultimum remedium to enhance access to justice of victims with a mental disability, in: *Brems / Desmet* (eds.), Integrated Human Rights in Practice: Rewriting Human Rights Decisions, p. 294.

254 Ibid, p. 298.

255 Ibid.

256 *Hodson*, NGOs and the Struggle for Human Rights in Europe, p. 61.

257 *Cliquennois / Champetier*, The Economic, Judicial and Political Influence Exerted by Private Foundations on Cases Taken by NGOs to the European Court of Human Rights: Inklings of a New Cold War'?, European Law Journal Vol. 22, p. 97.

impact on the Court.[258] Similar provisions can be found in Rule 44(2) of the Rules of the Court. Since 2006, human rights NGOs influence the execution of the Court's judgements by submitting communications to the Committee of Ministers during the supervision process of States' compliance review with the final judgements.[259] Those rules enable civil society to have an impact on ECtHR litigation; they do not create an "open flood gate for NGO participation",[260] but rather demonstrate the perseverance of NGOs to challenge accessibility restrictions and also the Court's power to establish such extended participation.[261] Besides these operational changes, NGOs' litigation certainly shapes the overall case law of the Court.[262] This cannot only lead to changes in European law, the strategic selection of issues in which to intervene can shape Europe's general human rights policy and further contributes to the juridification and judicialisation of the identified issues.[263]

In sum, despite the restrictions imposed by Article 34 ECHR ('victim status'), NGOs as litigators are able to act in diverse ways and have a direct impact of the implementation, reform and development of the Court's jurisprudence, the Convention and the overall European human rights regime. If replicated, this approach would be of particular relevance not only in regional systems but indeed influence domestic and international courts on a global scale as well.[264]

---

258 *Cliquennois / Champetier*, The Economic, Judicial and Political Influence Exerted by Private Foundations on Cases Taken by NGOs to the European Court of Human Rights: Inklings of a New Cold War'?, European Law Journal Vol. 22, p. 98.

259 Ibid; see also Rule 9.2 of the Rules of the Committee of Ministers for the supervision of the execution of judgements and of the terms of friendly settlements.

260 *Cichowski*, Civil Society and the European Court of Human Rights, in: *Christoffersen / Madsen* (eds.), The European Court of Human Rights between Law and Politics, p. 87.

261 Ibid.

262 *Cliquennois / Champetier*, The Economic, Judicial and Political Influence Exerted by Private Foundations on Cases Taken by NGOs to the European Court of Human Rights: Inklings of a New Cold War'?, European Law Journal Vol. 22, p. 125.

263 Ibid.

264 *Cichowski*, Civil Society and the European Court of Human Rights, in: *Christoffersen / Madsen* (eds.), The European Court of Human Rights between Law and Politics, p. 88.

# 4 Shrinking Space

Having elaborated the role of civil society in shaping human rights policy and the framework for the protection of HRDs, attention now turns to assess the adequacy of these protections. In particular the issue of 'shrinking space' needs further investigation. In this section, the shrinking space problem will be addressed with a particular focus on the European region. The following section builds on this analysis and offers new ideas to overcome the deficiencies identified, to effectively respond to violations of the rights of human rights defenders and to reverse the trend towards shrinking, or even closing space for civil society.

The term 'shrinking space,' in reference to civil society, has no universal definition: the attribute "shrinking" can be applied only depending on how the 'space' is defined. Some argue that it is only about the possibility to influence politics, whereas others consider it as space to operate, protest, criticise organize or express opinions as well as dissent.[265] The latter view reflects the space described in section 2, in which a vital civil society is able not just to act, but also be empowered, and thus the 'space' referred to in this thesis. When this space is subject to restrictions, it can be defined as "shrinking space". Constraints on space for civil society can be designed by various means and ranges: from restrictions on funding (by public and private donors or exclusion from the banking system), to limits barring the creation of CSOs; through smear campaigns and public defamation against HRDs; through refusing access to (inter-)national organisations; by restrictive laws and arbitrary bureaucratic burdens; up to repression, criminalization, illegal confinement enforced disappearance, and culminating in

265 *Hayes, et al.*, On "shrinking space" – a framing paper, *Twomey* (ed.), Transnational Institute, 2017, p. 3.

torture and killings of HRDs.[266] The global trend toward shrinking space entails such an immense volume and diversity of threats that it is difficult to tackle repression systematically and thus to effectively combat violations against HRDs.

To illustrate these partially abstract threats, a concrete example is the 2012 Russian NGO law, which requires foreign funded CSOs tasked with 'political activities' to register as 'foreign agents', a term with heavy negative connotations in Russia, as it is synonymous for foreign spies.[267] Similarly, Egypt has been referred to as the "innovator in the shrinking space phenomenon."[268] The government began its most recent efforts by freezing the funds and assets of domestic NGOs and HRDs and, later in 2014, even changed the penal code placing HRDs at risk of life-long imprisonment for accepting certain foreign funding.[269] Furthermore, after the alleged coup attempts in Turkey, the degree of freedom and democracy in the country "has been in free fall".[270] Among countless examples is the arbitrary detention of many HRDs like Taner Kılıç, the former Chair of Amnesty International Turkey and Osman Kavala, once the advisor of the Turkish government on the peace process between the Kurdistan Workers Party (PKK) and President Erdoğan's government.[271] Both face charges for alleged terrorist offences, despite the "absence of any material evidence that they

266 Cf. *Buyse*, Squeezing civic space: restrictions on civil society organizations and the linkage with human rights, The International Journal of Human Rights 2018 Vol. 22, No. 8, p. 966 ff.; Directorate-General for External Policies, Policy Department, Shrinking space for civil society: the EU response, 2017, p. 9ff.; *Eaton*, Human Rights Defenders in the United Nations Framework, 25 Hum. Rts. Defender 5, p. 5ff.; *Nah, et al.*, A Research Agenda for the Protection of Human Rights Defenders, Journal of Human Rights Practice, Volume 5, Issue 3, p. 402 ff.

267 *Buyse*, Squeezing civic space: restrictions on civil society organizations and the linkage with human rights, The International Journal of Human Rights 2018 Vol. 22, No. 8, p. 966.

268 Directorate-General for External Policies, Policy Department, Shrinking space for civil society: the EU response, 2017, p. 11.

269 Ibid.

270 Freedom House, Freedom in the World 2018 Democracy in Crisis, p. 7, https://freedomhouse.org/sites/default/files/FH_FITW_Report_2018_Final_SinglePage.pdf.

271 Amnesty International, Weathering the Storm – Defending Human Rights in Turkey's climate of fear, p. 5.

had indeed committed a recognisable criminal offense."[272] Such developments are, however, not limited to (semi-) authoritarian regimes, the global fight against terrorism induced several established democracies to take restrictive actions against NGOs in the name of good purposes.[273] It is observable that the discourse regarding anti-terror measures is premeditatedly abused to restrict and defame CSOs.[274] Arguments for such constraints are often that 'side effects' limiting fundamental rights and freedoms are necessary to maintain public security.[275] As Alston argues even more drastically: "*People are now widely convinced that security can only be achieved through making enormous trade-offs, whether in terms of freedom of movement, privacy, non-discrimination norms, or even personal integrity guarantees.*"[276] This might lead to the farcical idea that freedom and human rights can only be defended through restrictions on fundamental freedoms and rights. In other words, that it is necessary to restrict concrete fundamental rights in order to defend an abstract, overarching idea of freedom and democracy; an exercise in circular reasoning.

Freedom House, a NGO dedicated to monitoring civil and political liberties, noted in its 2018 annual world report, that a decade of worldwide decline in global freedom continues and announced the 12th consecutive year of recession.[277] In the last twelve years, far more countries incurred democratic setbacks than those that recorded gains.[278] Moreover, the former UN Special Rapporteur on the Rights to Freedom of Peaceful Assembly and of Association argues that it is almost behind the times to talk about shrinking civil space, because in many

---

272 Amnesty International, Weathering the Storm – Defending Human Rights in Turkey's climate of fear, p. 5.

273 *Buyse*, Squeezing civic space: restrictions on civil society organizations and the linkage with human rights, The International Journal of Human Rights 2018 Vol. 22, No. 8, p. 966.

274 *Kreienkamp*, Responding to the Global Crackdown on Civil Society, Global Governance Institute, Policy Brief September 2017, p. 5.

275 Ibid.

276 *Alston*, The Populist Challenge to Human Rights, Journal of Human Rights Practice Vol. 9, Issue 1, 2017, p. 4.

277 Freedom House, Freedom in the World 2018 Democracy in Crisis, p. 1.

278 Ibid.

parts of the world, the space is 'already gone'.[279] Beyond a mere trend, the "risks becoming the new norm."[280] Nonetheless, despite this recognition and attention at high levels, the empirical knowledge of repressive laws and actions against CSOs and HRDs remains low.[281] The previously mentioned Freedom House report gives initial hints about the general deteriorations of fundamental rights, it is, however, not undisputed.[282] Furthermore the report provides no specific data about constraints directly targeting civil society organizations.[283] More helpful in this regard, the United States Agency for International Development CSO Sustainability Index puts a particular focus on the civil society realm. The index allocates comparable data regarding the 'sustainability' of civil society including the analysis of the legal environment.[284] Although the availability of long-term data is limited and the index focuses on Central and Eastern Europe and Eurasia,[285] these limits do not impair the present analysis, in view of this thesis' scope. Two more efforts to document negative impacts on civil society worldwide are also noteworthy. Firstly, the International Centre for Not-for-Profit Law (ICNL) focuses on concrete legal limitations on CSOs. The ICNL assessed legal restrictions on CSOs enacted between 2012 and 2014, finding that 36% targeted funding, 19% restricted freedom of assembly and 45% concern the lifecycle or 'framework regulation' of CSOs, meaning their establishment, operation, dissolution, etcetera.[286] Secondly, the rather new CIVICUS Monitor, an up-to-date world map, re-

279 *Kiai*, Reclaiming Civic Space through U.N. Supported Litigation, SUR 22 – v.12 n.22, p. 246.

280 Ibid.

281 *Kreienkamp*, Responding to the Global Crackdown on Civil Society, Global Governance Institute, Policy Brief September 2017, p. 2.

282 The Report has been accused by some of political and ideological biased; cf. *Steiner*, Comparing Freedom House Democracy Scores to Alternative Indices and Testing for Political Bias: Are US Allies Rated More Democratic by Freedom House?, Journal of Comparative Policy Analysis: Research and Practice, Vol. 18 (4), pp. 329–349.

283 *Kreienkamp*, Responding to the Global Crackdown on Civil Society, Global Governance Institute, Policy Brief September 2017, p. 2.

284 Ibid.

285 Ibid.

286 *Kreienkamp*, Responding to the Global Crackdown on Civil Society, Global Governance Institute, Policy Brief September 2017, p. 7; *Rutzen*, Civil Society under Assault, Journal of Democracy, Vol. 26, No. 4, 2015, pp. 29 ff.

leased by CIVICUS, an international alliance of civil society representatives, which indicates the degree of free civic space globally. This non-exhaustive enumeration of reliable data resources illustrates the widespread discourse of the issue, revealing varying sources, methodologies, prioritisation and geographical and temporal purviews.[287] It also shows few achievements regarding a comprehensive overview on the restrictions and repression against civil society and its key players: NGOs and thereby human rights defenders. Common findings in all of the available databases are however the "pervasiveness of restrictions and the existence of regional patterns."[288] Those patterns suggest that States replicate neighbouring countries' repressive conduct, or have at least fewer inhibitions to act in such an oppressive way.[289] This might then lead to the conclusion that regional imitation is a significant aspect in order to elucidate how States respect and construe the international human rights system.[290]

The international human rights protection regime – comprised of different bodies, such as UN or EU agencies or international courts – can serve as a counterbalance to the shrinking space phenomena on national and international level.[291] The norms enshrined in international treaties are finally the "legal ropes of duty"[292] which bind the state and to which the international community voluntarily agreed. This body of IHRL and its institutions provide a clearer view on the specific issue of shrinking space. Going beyond circuitous, abstract debates, IHRL provides a framework to assess which rights are at risk, and understanding whether a violation has occurred.[293]

For the purpose of this work, since the legal and administrative restrictions, persecutions and other violations of universally recognized human rights of HRDs and civil society organisations are of particular

287 *Kreienkamp*, Responding to the Global Crackdown on Civil Society, Global Governance Institute, Policy Brief September 2017, p. 3.

288 Ibid.

289 Ibid.

290 Ibid.

291 *Buyse*, Squeezing civic space: restrictions on civil society organizations and the linkage with human rights, The International Journal of Human Rights 2018 Vol. 22, No. 8, p. 978.

292 Ibid.

293 Ibid.

interest, they are discussed in more detail below. The principal focus, remains on the European region, which is of considerable interest, in view of the regional imitation effect referenced above.

## 4.1 States Crack-Down on Civil Society and Human Rights Defenders Within Europe

Europe as part of the world with the "lion's share of countries with 'open' civic space"[294] is undergoing a transformation towards closing civil space. While the issue was primarily considered a predicament of the Global South, recent negative developments in terms of promoting and protecting human rights and democratic values, which fit in the characterization of 'shrinking space', are perceived in the Global North and thus also in Europe.[295] Particularly – though not only- in the east of Europe, countries such as Hungary or Poland and of course, with regard to CoE members, Azerbaijan, Russia and Turkey have established repressive policies. But not only have the obvious actors cracked-down on civil society, civic space in the United Kingdom (UK) is currently rated as 'narrowed' due to counter-extremism laws, which have "negative consequences on associational life, and around violent policing tactics in the management of public assemblies."[296] A similar situation can be found in France, where the same rating ("narrowed") is applied as consequence of the state of emergency imposed in 2015 and its repercussions (restrictions on freedom of expression and of peaceful assembly).[297] While there might be reasons for weighing such restrictions, the negative impacts on fundamental rights as consequence of restrictive policies regarding freedom of expression and assembly have to be taken in consideration. Regarding the EU, of the hitherto28

294 Quoted from: *Kreienkamp*, Responding to the Global Crackdown on Civil Society, Global Governance Institute, Policy Brief September 2017, p. 4.

295 *Cernov*, Civil Society is not the Enemy, Sur – 26 – v.14 n.26, 2017, p. 50.

296 CIVICUS, Monitor 2016, https://monitor.civicus.org/newsfeed/2016/09/01/united-kingdom-overview/.

297 CIVICUS, Monitor 2016, https://monitor.civicus.org/newsfeed/2016/09/01/france-overview/.

member States,[298] 13 obtained the rating of "narrowed" or even "obstructed" civic space.[299] In a union, essentially based on fundamental freedoms and democracy, those developments are alarming. On a larger scale, including the CoE members Turkey and Russia, it is determined that those two semi-democratic countries in particular are targeting the free flow of information, repressing freedom of expression and thus are considered as "some of the most dangerous countries for journalists (outside of war zones)."[300] Regarding the lessening civic space, the most crucial fundamental rights which are violated seem to be freedom of peaceful assembly, freedom of expression the freedom of association and furthermore the restriction of funding. At a first glance the latter could appear as not necessarily a fundamental right; however it is in opposition with the wording provided in Article 13 of the UN Declaration, Paragraph 13 EU Guidelines and Paragraphs 70 to 73 of the OSCE Guidelines. Moreover, the individual HRDs oftentimes risk their lives and thus, the right to life is an issue as well. Hence, the mentioned rights are most at stake globally and will therefore be examined in the following paragraphs, concentrating on Europe.

### 4.1.1 Threats to Physical Integrity

Physical integrity, and thus the right to life and the prohibition of torture and other ill-treatment, as listed in Articles 2 and 3 ECHR (and also in Articles 6 and 7 ICCPR) are among the main guarantees for people under the ECtHR's jurisdiction and one of the main duties of States in the human rights protection regime. Article 12 (2) of the UN Declaration adopted those rights and framed them as following:

> "*State*[s] *shall take all necessary measures to ensure the protection by the competent authorities of everyone, individually and in association with others, against any violence, threats, retaliation, de facto or de jure adverse dis-*

298 After a referendum from 23 June 2016, The United Kingdom is expected to leave the EU on 29 March 2019.

299 CIVICUS Monitor, People Power Under Attack – A Global Analysis of Threats to Fundamental Freedoms, 2018, p. 28.

300 *Kreienkamp*, Responding to the Global Crackdown on Civil Society, Global Governance Institute, Policy Brief September 2017, p. 8.

*crimination, pressure or any other arbitrary action as a consequence of his or her legitimate exercise of the rights referred to in the present Declaration.*"

In the past, governments often simply killed those who criticized its governance or human rights compliance.[301] Nowadays, it is more common to hide such assassinations and conveniently declare 'unknown assailants' as perpetrators.[302] While those practices are well documented for instance in Kenya, Sri Lanka or Colombia[303] they also occur under the umbrella of the ECHR.

For instance, the case of Daphne Caruana Galizia, an investigative Maltese journalist killed in 2017 by a bomb planted in her car. She was known for criticising the government and for having reported about political corruption. Although three suspects have been charged with her assassination, it is assumed that it was a contract killing and the backers behind the crime are still unidentified.[304] Furthermore, Tahir Elçi, a Pro-Kurdish lawyer who was first detained by the Turkish police, later charged for allegedly making terrorist propaganda and finally publicly shot whilst making a press statement,[305] falls into this category. Not only the investigation of the killing was questionable, but Tahir Elci's widow received a text message at the funeral, supposedly from a police officer, saying "You are next".[306] The investigations stalled and even today, no progress has been reached, a fact that is heavily criticized by civil society.[307] Another case was the abduction and murder of human rights defender Natalia Estemirova, a researcher and investiga-

301 *Roth*, The Abuser's Reaction: Intensifying Attacks on Human Rights Defenders, Orgnizations, and Institutions, 16 Brown J. World Aff. 15, 2010, p. 16.

302 Ibid, p. 17.

303 Ibid, pp. 17 ff.

304 Freedom House, Freedom in the World 2018: The Annual Survey of Political Rights and Civil Liberties, p. 614.

305 *Yeginsu*, Prominent Kurdish Lawyer Is Killed in Southeast Turkey, The New York Times, 28 November 2015, https://www.nytimes.com/2015/11/29/world/europe/turkey-kurds-tahir-elci-killed-in-sur.html.

306 *Gardner*, At the Funeral of Tahir Elci a giant in Turkey's Human Rights Movement, the sense of loss is deafening, 30 November 2015, https://www.amnesty.org/en/latest/news/2015/11/at-the-funeral-of-tahir-elci-a-giant-in-turkeys-human-rights-movement-the-sense-of-loss-is-deafening/.

307 Stockholm Center for Freedom, Turkish gov't covers up killing of lawyer, human rights activist Tahir Elçi, https://stockholmcf.org/turkish-govt-covers-up-killing-of-lawyer-human-rights-activist-tahir-elci/.

tor for the Russian human rights NGO, 'Memorial'. Many cases investigated by Ms. Estemirova against Russia were brought before the ECtHR and oftentimes the Court found violations of the ECHR by the State.[308]

While the first two examples are quite difficult to bring before an international court, so long as the States keep up appearances of compliance with the rule of law, the latter case of Natalia Estemirova was brought before the ECtHR.[309] Although, there are many cases brought before the Court against Russia in the context of gross violations against HRDs in the North Caucasus region, especially in Chechnya,[310] the case of Natalia Estemirova is of particular interest. Not only because of the severe human rights violations directly aimed against an HRD and her work, but also because of the third-party intervention under Article 36 ECHR (as discussed above in paragraph 3.2.2.4) by the Council of Europe's Commissioner for Human Rights.[311]

Natalia Estemirova, the leading member of "leading NGO documenting human rights violations in the North Caucasus"[312] was highly acknowledged as an HRD both nationally as well as internationally. She was abducted near her home in Grozny (Chechnya) on 15 July 2009, as observed by two witnesses.[313] Later that day, her dead body (shots to her head and chest) was found in the neighbouring Republic of Ingushetia.[314] The case was then investigated by the authorities, who as of yet have not been able to find justice for her. Her relatives and their lawyers filed several complaints in the investigation, claiming to re-

308 Cf. *Musayeva and Others v. Russia*, no. 74239/01, judgement of 26 July 2007; *Alikhadzhiyeva v. Russia*, no. 68007/01, judgement of 5 July 2007; *Makayeva v. Russia*, no. 37287/09, judgement of 18 September 2014.

309 *Estemirova v. Russia*, no. 42705/11, lodged on 21 June 2011, statement of facts.

310 Cf. *Van der Vet*, Transitional Justice in Chechnya: NGO Political Advocacy for Implementing Chechen Judgments of the European Court of Human Rights, Review of Central and East European Law 38, 2013, pp. 368 ff.

311 Third Party Intervention by the Council of Europe Commissioner for Human Rights, Application No. 42705/11 Svetlana Khusainovna ESTEMIROVA against the Russian Federation, 14 March 2016, CommDH(2016)18.

312 Ibid, p. 9, § 30.

313 *Estemirova v. Russia*, no. 42705/11, lodged on 21 June 2011, statement of facts, pp. 2 f.

314 Ibid, p. 3.

ceive access to crucial documents regarding the murder, which was partly granted. However, due to tactical purposes, insight to the entire case file was denied. Their complaints against this were finally dismissed by the Supreme Court of the Chechen Republic in December 2010.[315] The victim's sister, Svetlana Khusainovna Estemirova, lodged an application before the ECtHR, claiming a violation of Articles 2 and 13 of the ECHR citing the murder of her sister and the failure of public authorities to conduct an effective, fast and thorough investigation of her death.[316] Available evidence suggests that State officials are possibly involved in the events: personal threats against Ms Estemirova from State agents and – as validated by ECtHR judgements – systemic, extrajudicial killings, ill-treatments and enforced disappearances committed by the State's security forces happened in the region since 1999.[317] Moreover, Ms. Estemirova was allegedly threatened by the President of the Chechen Republic, Mr. Kadyrov, who personally said that "he [had had] blood on his hands and that he had killed before and would continue killing bad people and that he [had not been] ashamed of it."[318] Another striking indication is that her body was found in the neighbouring Republic of Ingushetia where it was at this time not possible to freely cross the border without being checked by government controlled road checkpoints.[319] Finally, the complaint is summed up in Amnesty International's findings regarding State impunity in Chechnya:

> "*There has been an almost total failure of political will to uphold the rule of law and address impunity for present and past abuses of human rights in the region. Those responsible for abuses walk free while victims and their families have no redress through the Russian judicial system*"[320]

After filling the application to the ECtHR, the CoE's Commissioner of Human Rights, Nils Muižnieks, intervened as a third party in the case

315 *Estemirova v. Russia*, no. 42705/11, lodged on 21 June 2011, statement of facts, pp. 2–4.
316 Ibid, p. 6.
317 Ibid, p. 5.
318 Ibid.
319 Ibid, p. 4.
320 Amnesty International, Rule without law: Human rights violations in the North Caucasus, July 2009, AI Index: EUR 46/012/2009.

and submitted his written observations to the Court. He emphasised the "persistent patterns of impunity for serious human rights violations"[321] in the region and clarified his mandate under Article 36 (3) ECHR and under the Declaration of the Committee of Ministers on Council of Europe action to improve the protection of human rights defenders and promote their activities, which states that the Commissioner is invited "to strengthen the role and capacity of his Office in order to provide strong and effective protection for human rights defenders."[322] The Commissioner insistently drew attention the severe corrosive effects of impunity regarding the fundamental principles of a democratic society.[323] The climate of threats and lethal violence specifically targeting HRDs results in general chilling effects and significantly reduces the possibility for independent human rights work.[324] Thus, not only HRDs themselves are at risk, their capacity to help victims of human rights violations, including filing complaints before the ECtHR is seriously undermined.

In his overall appraisal, the Commissioner found that Russia's government agencies "have failed to prevent and to react appropriately to the most serious human rights violations against human rights defenders in the North Caucasus region."[325] The case of Natalia Estemirova should moreover not be considered an isolated one, indeed it is part of a larger pattern of threatening and killing HRDs in the region.[326]

Through this elaboration, it becomes clear that even severe human rights violations directly targeting HRDs because of their work occur

321 Third Party Intervention by the Council of Europe Commissioner for Human, Application No. 42705/11 Svetlana Khusainovna ESTEMIROVA against the Russian Federation, 14 March 2016, CommDH(2016)18, § 4.

322 Ibid, § 3; Council of Europe, Declaration of the Committee of Ministers on Council of Europe action to improve the protection of human rights defenders and promote their activities, 6 February 2008.

323 Council of Europe, Declaration of the Committee of Ministers on Council of Europe action to improve the protection of human rights defenders and promote their activities, 6 February 2008, para. 7.

324 Third Party Intervention by the Council of Europe Commissioner for Human, Application No. 42705/11 Svetlana Khusainovna ESTEMIROVA against the Russian Federation, 14 March 2016, CommDH(2016)18, § 29.

325 Ibid, § 35.

326 Ibid, § 34.

in CoE member states. Despite the protection mechanism under the ECHR, many infringements remain unpunished. This is especially apparent when states pretend to investigate crimes and allegedly stick to the rule of law – as illustrated in the cases above – while in the meantime, passing restrictive laws targeting NGOs and thus do not provide a safe and enabling environment for civil society. This highlights the importance of third-party interventions and thereby also the importance of involvement from NGOs and other human rights actors in the ECtHR's litigation. Where particularly vulnerable people are involved, NGO involvement is even more important. The example of Ms. Estemirova illustrates the consequences when standards cumulated in the UN Declaration, namely Articles 2, 9 and 12, are abandoned. Equally, the case illustrates the reasonable and clear line of the UN Declaration and demonstrates that an implementation of and adherence to those standards could have prevented such violations or at least could have afforded an effective remedy.

The interaction of denying a safe legal environment, adopting restrictive NGO laws and violating fundamental rights, will be further illustrated in the following paragraphs.

### 4.1.2 Restrictions on Freedom of Association and Funding

Freedom of association is not only intertwined with freedom of expression and assembly, it is, in the present context, also interwoven with restrictions on funding and other restrictive NGO laws. The UN Declaration elaborated this coherent framework in Articles 5–9, 11–13 and 17. The great importance of the right to freedom of association is reflected in its international dissemination and acceptance as one of the fundamental principles of democracy and respect for human rights. Articles 20 UDHR, 22 (1) ICCPR, 8 ICESCR, 16 ACHR and Article 11 (1) ECHR all guarantee freedom of association, as reiterated in Article 5 UN Declaration on Human Rights Defenders. Restrictions on the exercise of this right, as already discussed in paragraph 3.2.2.3, ought not to be imposed, except for those grounds which are prescribed by law, serve a legitimate aim and which are necessary in a democratic society. Under European law the following are considered legitimate aims: national security interests; protection of public safety, public health or morals; prevention of disorder or crime; and protection of the rights and freedoms of others.[327]

In the present context, restrictions on funding and other restrictive NGO laws have significant implications for freedom of association. As noted, registration is vitally important for NGOs, as it is often linked with granting rights and benefits, such as legal personality.[328] Moreover, in some states it is mandatory to register, making normal NGO operations without state approval impossible.[329] Although they can effectively paralyse crucial civil society institutions, restrictions on funding and other oppressive regulations on NGOs are not clearly regulated in international law. The UN Special Rapporteur on the Rights to Freedom of Peaceful Assembly and of Association noted, in accordance with Article 13 of the UN Declaration on Human Rights Defenders, that no restriction on associations' (whether registered or not) funding shall be made, including from external sources, when access to associations and thus the freedom of association would be restricted.[330] A substantial element of freedom of association is the capacity to "seek, secure and use financial resources from domestic, foreign and international sources."[331] Only under the high preconditions with the strong justifications for restricting the right, as discussed above, could such limitations be lawful. Therefore, restrictions on funding and laws constraining the establishment of NGOs can fall within the scope of protection of freedom of association and hence must pass the 'necessity-test'. In this regard it is advisable to base the assumption that freedom is the rule, and restrictions can only be the exception.[332] However, many states, in the European region as well, curtail access to funding

327 OSCE, Guidelines on the Protection of Human Rights Defenders, p. 88.

328 *Buyse*, Squeezing civic space: restrictions on civil society organizations and the linkage with human rights, The International Journal of Human Rights 2018 Vol. 22, No. 8, p. 970.

329 Ibid.

330 A/HRC/23/39, 24 April 2013, Report of the Special Rapporteur on the rights to freedom of peaceful assembly and of association, Maina Kiai, paras. 17–18, 79 and 82.

331 OSCE, Guidelines on the Protection of Human Rights Defenders, p. 98.

332 A/HRC/23/39, 24 April 2013, Report of the Special Rapporteur on the rights to freedom of peaceful assembly and of association, Maina Kiai, para. 18.

for NGOs significantly. This is conducted with various methods: adapting new laws or normative decrees and regulations such as heavy bureaucratic requirements to register as an NGO, imposing considerably complicated financial reporting demands or other authorization obligations which must be granted by the state.[333]

For better illustration, the following cases demonstrate concretely the close relationship between freedom of association, restrictions on funding and enacting of repressive NGO laws. At least since 2005, Russia has generally pursued a course to fight NGOs, especially those critical of the government or advocating human rights. In 2012 the State Duma passed law No. 121-FZ, better known as the 'foreign agent law,' in order to limit the scope of action for NGOs receiving foreign funding and engaging in political activities.[334] This piece of law has not only negatively affected the entire range of civil, cultural and human rights organizations, but it can furthermore be considered as a blueprint for other oppressive laws adopted in neighbouring countries in the region – the 'copycat-effect' discussed previously. The 'foreign agent law' is, however, nothing astonishing. Rather, it is just the current state of a longer process towards a repressive climate of fear amongst HRDs and their organizations.[335] The wording in the law, that organizations are not entitled to work against national interests, security or public order, became a popular catch phrase, repeated new legislations by various countries; likely because this particular formulation is rather broad and thus opens the scope for interpretation, and can therefore easily be tweaked.[336] The imitation effect has spread even to the European Union, as best observed in Hungary. The Act LXXVI of 2017 on the Transparency of Organisations Supported from Abroad, known as the 'Anti-NGO-Law' is similar to the Russian role model, targeting NGOs that obtain foreign funding. Those organisations are required to label themselves in every fora (publications, websites, etcetera) as recipients

333 OSCE, Guidelines on the Protection of Human Rights Defenders, p. 98.

334 *Van der Vet / Lyytikäinenb*, Violence and human rights in Russia: how human rights defenders develop their tactics in the face of danger, 2005–2013, The International Journal of Human Rights, Vol. 19 No. 7, 2015, p. 979.

335 Ibid, pp. 981 ff.

336 *Unmüßig*, Civil society under pressure – shrinking – closing – no space, Heinrich Böll Foundation, Berlin, May 2016, p. 8.

of foreign funds.[337] In addition, the identity of every financial backer shall be disclosed and non-compliance entails severe fines or even liquidation.[338] The emphasis on the donor's identities became explicit after a major campaign by the Hungarian government, wherein Hungarian Prime Minister Orban actually discredited NGOs as foreign paid activists, interfering in internal political affairs in order to pursue external interests,[339] leading the law to be labelled the 'Stop Soros Law.'[340] Such attacks are often used to publicly discredit and defame HRDs and their work. Similar developments have also been recently monitored in Poland. Just as Hungary, the Polish government incited anti-immigrant sentiments and then passed new administrative proceedings regarding funding of NGOs, especially targeting those involved in migration issues and refugee aid.[341] This is frequently conducted with the usually specious reasoning on the grounds of fighting terrorism and combating money laundering.[342]

In the Hungarian case, on the same day the law was passed, Amnesty International characterized it as "a vicious and calculated assault on civil society"[343] and many Hungarian organizations heavily criticised it as "unnecessary, stigmatising and harmful".[344] Besides this predictable uproar from NGOs, the law also caught the attention of European bodies. The CoE and EU institutions called for reconsideration or withdrawal of the law and the European Commission for Democracy through Law (the Venice Commission), an advisory body staffed with constitutional law specialists, began reviewing the law on demand of

337 *Buyse*, Squeezing civic space: restrictions on civil society organizations and the linkage with human rights, The International Journal of Human Rights 2018 Vol. 22, No. 8, p. 979.

338 Ibid.

339 Ibid.

340 The legislation is named after the Hungarian-American investor and philanthropist George Soros, who is constantly denounced for his civic engagement by rightwing governments worldwide.

341 *Kapronczay*, War on NGOs in Eastern Europe, SUR 26 – v.14 n.26, p. 111.

342 Ibid, p. 112.

343 Amnesty International, Hungary: NGO law a vicious and calculated assault on civil society, Press Release, 13 June 2017.

344 OSCE Office for Democratic Institutions and Human Rights (ODIHR), Independent Civil Society Under Attack in Hungary – Statement by Hungarian NGOs, 22 September 2017 https://www.osce.org/odihr/339316?download=true.

the CoE's Parliamentary Assembly.[345] The Venice Commission reached the conclusion that the law caused "disproportionate and unnecessary interference with the freedoms of association and expression, the right to privacy, and the prohibition of discrimination."[346] Thereafter, the European Commission started infringement proceedings against the country and found that the new rules assail the freedom of association and also "the rights to protection of private life and personal data, as protected in the Charter of Fundamental Rights of the European Union, and was discriminatory."[347] In Hungary, an association of 23 organisations challenged the law before the Constitutional Court.[348] Analogous developments can be witnessed with regard to the role model of all these regulations, the Russian 'foreign agent law'. The European Human Rights Advocacy Centre (EHRAC), in the name of a consortium of civil society actors (now 49 applications in total), filed a 'collective complaint' to the ECtHR, challenging the legality of the Russian law under Articles 10 and 11 ECHR.[349] This challenge made an effort to fight for free civil space in Russia.[350] However, while the cases were already lodged in 2013, it took four years to communicate them to Russia, even though the CoE's Commissioner for Human Rights had al-

345 *Buyse*, Squeezing civic space: restrictions on civil society organizations and the linkage with human rights, The International Journal of Human Rights 2018 Vol. 22, No. 8, p. 979.

346 Venice Commission, Hungary: Opinion on the Draft Law on the Transparency of Organisations Receiving Support from Abroad, CDL-REF(2017)015, 20 June 2017, para. 64.

347 *Buyse*, Squeezing civic space: restrictions on civil society organizations and the linkage with human rights, The International Journal of Human Rights 2018 Vol. 22, No. 8, pp. 979 f.

348 Ibid, p. 980.

349 *Ecodefence and others against Russia and 48 other applications*, Application no. 9988/13, Communicated on 22 March 2017.

350 *Buyse*, Squeezing civic space: restrictions on civil society organizations and the linkage with human rights, The International Journal of Human Rights 2018 Vol. 22, No. 8, p. 980.

ready condemned the law in 2013[351] and 2015,[352] as had the Venice Commission in 2014,[353] the Human Rights Resource Centre in 2015 and Amnesty International in 2016.[354] Moreover, in 2017 the Commissioner for Human Rights intervened as third party in the case,[355] just as the International Commission of Jurists, together with Amnesty International, did in the same year[356]. Finally, at the beginning of 2018 EHRAC replied to the Russian Government Observations.[357] These numerous institutions all concluded that the passed Act by the Russian government contravenes human rights guaranteed under the ECHR.[358] The Commissioner for Human Rights argued that the law implements "unjustified discriminatory treatment for a particular set of organisations"[359] and thereby interfered with the right to freedom of association enforced through the requirement that NGOs self-label as

351 Council of Europe, Opinion of the Commissioner for Human Rights on the Legislation of the Russian Federation on Non-Commercial Organisations in Light of Council of Europe Standards, CommDH(2013) 15, 15 July 2013.

352 Council of Europe, Opinion of the Commissioner for Human Rights on the Legislation of the Russian Federation on Non-Commercial Organisations in Light of Council of Europe Standards: an Update, CommDH(2015)17, 9 July 2015.

353 Venice Commission, Opinion on "Law on Foreign Agents" and "Law on Treason" of the Russian Federation CDL-AD(2014)025, 27 June 2014.

354 *Bowring*, The Crisis of the European Court of Human Rights in the Face of Authoritarian and Populist Regimes in: *Kent et al.* (eds.), The Future of International Courts, Chapter 5, p. 14.

355 Third Party Intervention by the Council of Europe Commissioner for Human, Application no. 9988/13, Ecodefence and others against Russia and 48 other applications.

356 Written Submissions on Behalf of the International Commission of Jurists (ICJ) and Amnesty International, Application no. 9988/13, Ecodefence and others against Russia and 48 other applications, 2 October 2017.

357 *Bowring*, The Crisis of the European Court of Human Rights in the Face of Authoritarian and Populist Regimes in: *Kent et al.* (eds.), The Future of International Courts, Chapter 5, p. 14.

358 Third Party Intervention by the Council of Europe Commissioner for Human, Application no. 9988/13, Ecodefence and others against Russia and 48 other applications, p. 10, paras. 38–44; Written Submissions on Behalf of the International Commission of Jurists (ICJ) and Amnesty International, Application no. 9988/13, Ecodefence and others against Russia and 48 other applications, 2 October 2017, p. 9.

359 Third Party Intervention by the Council of Europe Commissioner for Human, Application no. 9988/13, Ecodefence and others against Russia and 48 other applications, para. 12.

'foreign agent', the broad and loose wording of the term 'political activity' to bring organisations under the scope of the law, and the disproportionate – and even criminal – charges for non-compliance with the restrictive regulations.[360] Although the case is still pending, the interventions increase the general public attention regarding the case and the attempts to shrink civil space.

The given examples highlight the implications for freedom of association of oppressive laws and regulations regarding registration and funding of NGOs. Especially in the guise of anti-terrorism measures or money laundering regulations, governments are attempting to silence critics of their activities or labelling important commitments to protect human rights as foreign interference in domestic affairs. It is undeniable that the aforementioned grounds of national security or public safety are legitimate aims for limitations of freedom of association, but this has to be in compliance with IHRL. Thus, restrictions must not merely pursue a legitimate aim but must be in conformity with international law, and must also be necessary for achieving this aim and proportionate to it.[361] As the UN Special on the Rights to Freedom of Peaceful Assembly and of Association evinces just suppressing opposition or justification of repressive practices may result in not passing the 'necessity test'.[362] Furthermore he stated that "[l]aws drafted in general terms limiting, or even banning funding under the justification of counter-terrorism do not comply with the requisites of 'proportionality' and 'necessity'."[363]

360 Third Party Intervention by the Council of Europe Commissioner for Human, Application no. 9988/13, Ecodefence and others against Russia and 48 other applications, para. 12.

361 OSCE, Guidelines on the Protection of Human Rights Defenders, p. 99; A/HRC/23/39, 24 April 2013, Report of the Special Rapporteur on the rights to freedom of peaceful assembly and of association, Maina Kiai para. 22.

362 A/HRC/23/39, 24 April 2013, Report of the Special Rapporteur on the rights to freedom of peaceful assembly and of association, Maina Kiai, para. 23.

363 Ibid.

### 4.1.3 Restrictions on Freedom of Expression and Freedom of Peaceful Assembly

Freedom of opinion and expression as it is recognized inter alia in Articles 19 UDHR, 19 ICCPR, 13 ACHR and 10 ECHR are "necessary condition[s] for the realization of the principles of transparency and accountability that are, in turn, essential for the promotion and protection of human rights."[364] Freedom of peaceful assembly (Articles 20 UDHR, 21 ICCPR, 15 ACHR and 11 ECCHR) is "a fundamental right in a democratic society and, like the right to freedom of expression, one of the foundations of such society"[365]. This already highlights the close connection between freedom of expression and peaceful assembly and they are even more intertwined in the discussion on HRDs' rights. As the ECtHR often pointed out, Article 11 ECHR must be interpreted in the light of Article 10 ECHR and *vice versa*,[366] as, in the Court's view, "the protection of opinions and the freedom to express them [...] [is] one of the objectives of freedom of assembly."[367] Those connections are also emphasized in the UN Declaration on HRDs, as the sequential Articles 5, 6 and 7 merging the international accepted norms regarding freedom of expression, inclusive of the right to receive information and communicate with international human rights bodies and to peacefully assemble. Thus, it seems appropriate to amalgamate them under one point.

Despite this unambiguous scope of protection[368] and the also, only under strict preconditions (legitimate aim, proportional, necessary in a democratic society), possibility to restrict the rights, many states impose arbitrary legal and administrative regulations impinging on these freedoms. Some states adopt such general norms that relevant procedures to comply with are unforeseeable; others provide excessive pow-

364 UN Human Rights Committee, General Comment No. 34 on Article 19, CCPR/C/GC/34, para. 3.

365 *Djavit An v. Turkey*, no. 20652/92, 20 February 2003, § 56.

366 *Schabas*, The European Convention on Human Rights: A Commentary, p. 492.

367 *Harris / O'Boyle / Warbrick*, Law of the European Convention on Human Rights, p. 711.

368 Cf. *Marauhn*, Freedom of Expression, Freedom of Assembly and Association, in: *Ehlers* (ed.), European Fundamental Rights and Freedoms, p. 98.

er to authorities to regulate assemblies beforehand and during demonstrations.[369] Thus, HRDs are often unable to organize such events due to immense administrative burdens or, even worse, content-based restrictions that fall within the scope of protection of freedom of assembly and expression. However, such blanket, content-based limitations are incompatible with international law.[370] Azerbaijan for example – despite being under the ECtHR's jurisdiction, – combined all the negative practices mentioned. As was examined in paragraph 3.2.2.3, Azerbaijan introduced several restrictive laws regarding NGOs with elements targeting HRDs in particular. Worth-mentioning here is the case *Mahammad Majidli v. Azerbaijan*[371] and three related cases, the proceedings for which were merged by the court.[372] In this context, the UN Special Rapporteur on the Rights to Freedom of Peaceful Assembly and of Association together with the Human Rights Centre of Ghent University lodged a joint third-party intervention in all four cases before the ECtHR.[373] Again, the importance of third party interventions, and thus, the part of civil society and also the correlation between different international and regional bodies, is evident. The interveners urged the Court to take solid steps in order to protect the fundamental rights compiled in the Convention. In the cases, the applicants were members of opposition parties who tried to organize demonstrations in Baku, the capital of Azerbaijan.[374] The applicants stated that they had no violent intentions and only called for "free and fair elections, right to freedom of assembly and democratic reforms in the

369 OSCE, Guidelines on the Protection of Human Rights Defenders, p. 79.

370 Ibid, pp. 80 f.

371 *Mahammad Majidli v. Azerbaijan application* Applications Nos. 24508/11 and 44581/13, judgement of 16 Fevruary 2017.

372 Mahammad Majidli v. Azerbaijan (no. 3) and three other applications application Nos. 56317/11, 67932/11, 27472/12 and 59661/12, Communicated on 2 July 2015.

373 Joint Third Party Intervention by The United Nations Special Rapporteur on the Rights to Freedom of Peaceful Assembly and of Associations and The Human Rights Centre of Ghent University, Mahammad Majidli v. Azerbaijan (no. 3) and three other applications application Nos. 56317/11, 67932/11, 27472/12 and 59661/12.

374 *Mahammad MAJIDLI v. Azerbaijan Application no 56317/11 and 3 other applications,* Communicated on 2 July 2015, § 1.

country, and were protesting against politically motivated arrests."[375] However, the demonstrations were not 'authorized' and several participants were arrested.[376] In this respect it is important to remember that Azerbaijan's national law, under amendments in 2016, restricts the right to assembly, if the assembly violates "public order and morals".[377] This is a critical point, as the wording is extensively broad and opens the floodgates for arbitrary restrictions, due to its large margin of interpretation.

The third-party interveners find, that "[t]he right to freedom of assembly is in a crisis in Azerbaijan, as is the situation of human rights defenders and civil society organizations, generally."[378] A major concern is the, by the state, established 'authorization regime,'[379] which imposes a pre-test the applicants must pass and which is often used by the state to criminalize participation in gatherings condemned by authorities. "Requiring authorization turns the right into a privilege to be dispensed by authorities."[380] This leads to an unlawful *reverse onus* as the burden of authorities to justify restrictions shifts beforehand into a burden on the organizers to refute theoretical grounds for rejection. The third-party interveners concluded that "the Government of Azerbaijan has moved beyond merely discouraging or chilling the right to freedom of peaceful assembly: It has effectively annihilated it."[381]

In light of Article 12 (2) UN Declaration on HRDs, States must take all requisite measures in order to protect the right to freedom of assembly against every threat, *de facto* or *de jure*, adverse discrimination, or other arbitrary action which, by implication, entails not adopting legisla-

---

375 *Mahammad MAJIDLI v. Azerbaijan Application no 56317/11 and 3 other applications*, Communicated on 2 July 2015, § 1.

376 Ibid.

377 Freedom House, Freedom in the World 2018: The Annual Survey of Political Rights and Civil Liberties, p. 40.

378 Joint Third Party Intervention by The United Nations Special Rapporteur on the Rights to Freedom of Peaceful Assembly and of Associations and The Human Rights Centre of Ghent University, Mahammad Majidli v. Azerbaijan (no. 3) and three other applications application Nos. 56317/11, 67932/11, 27472/12 and 59661/12, para. 21.

379 Ibid, paras. 9–11.

380 Ibid, para. 10.

381 Ibid, para. 23.

tion criminalizing the legitimate work of HRDs. The right to freedom of assembly and freedom of expression must be similarly secured, even if the gathering aims to "challenge traditional values, or [...] contest extreme political views."[382] Furthermore, substantive limitations on opinions expressed during a demonstration are only lawful when the high threshold of necessity established by the ECtHR is met.[383] The scope of interpretation of 'public order and morals,' laid down in the Azerbaijani law is very likely too broad to comply with this criterion.

## 4.2 Recapitulation of Shortcomings and how to Confront them

As has become apparent in the examples illuminated above, even under the jurisdiction of one of the world's best human rights protection systems, gross violations of fundamental rights not only occur, the safeguards, protectors and watchdogs for human rights – namely human rights defenders and the organizations they are working in – become the targets of attacks, solely on the basis of their work: standing up to protect human rights and defend democracy. These developments may not be new, but recent trends toward the expansion of policies targeting human rights advocates through the so-called 'copycat-effect' – even in former liberal and mostly democratic states – are alarming. Thus, the key shortcomings in the international legal protective regime regarding HRDs must be identified and tackled.

Unambiguously identifiable shortcomings are: the trends to pass restrictive laws that make it difficult for NGOs to register or to receive funding; public defamation of HRDs, even accusing them to be terrorists – all while justifying repression against the opposition as counter-terrorism or even assassinations attributed to 'unknown assailants'. However, the most important issue to address is the lack of implementation and effective enforcement of already established norms. By strengthening such rules, the 'toolbox' of instruments offered by IHRL could provide effective means to combat the recently established hostile climate for HRDs and their organizations. While the (non-ex-

382 OSCE, Guidelines on the Protection of Human Rights Defenders, p. 82.

383 Ibid, p. 81.

haustive) examples of human rights violations examined above in connection with HRDs and their work are well documented and various actors ranging from civil society organisations up to CoE officials raise great concerns about these developments, it is disenchanting that often no consequences follow. Impunity (as shown in the Case of Natalia Estemirova) can have a chilling-effect on all aspects of human rights protection. Even though Russia, when judged by the ECtHR, often pays compensation, the government continuously rejects implementation of the imposed structural reforms to end impunity.[384] Impunity for perpetrators of human rights violations on one side and the criminalization of HRDs and civil society organizations on the other, initiate a downward spiral which leads to a hostile environment for HRDs and their organizations. The ECHR however, if properly applied, can, at least for the European region, address both impunity and attempts to criminalize HRDs. The Convention, as a 'living instrument' contains no extensive catalogue of basic rights but rather selective fundamental rights, complemented by various additional protocols.[385] This structure of a living instrument ensures no theoretical or illusory rights, but provides a practical and effective human rights protection framework through dynamic interpretation capabilities by means of applicability to present developments.[386] Consequently, non-compliance with the Court's judgements undermines this protection regime severely. The international rule of law and international bodies are recently under attack, even by former supporters. As shown in this study, Poland, Azerbaijan, even the UK and certain other states have vanishing affection for the ECtHR, while Turkey and Russia are practically mere impassive members.[387] Those developments must strongly be countered.

In order to achieve a safe and enabling environment it is necessary to develop a holistic approach. This includes more collection and analysis of empirical data. As was pointed out in the previous paragraphs, there are indeed several actors who are analysing the issue of shrinking space from different angles, but there is still no comprehensive and –

384 *Roth*, The Abuser's Reaction: Intensifying Attacks on Human Rights Defenders, Orgnizations, and Institutions, 16 Brown J. World Aff. 15, 2010, p. 25.

385 *Von Arnauld*, Völkerrecht, p. 291.

386 Ibid.

387 *Alston*, Human Rights Under Siege, SUR 25 – v.14n.25, p. 269.

especially – valid evaluation of such findings. Oftentimes, the problem is the different methodological, temporal, geographical and textural approach used. The results of shortcomings are not comprehensively represented in the existing data sources and thus a solid empirical base is not available. Further research in this regard is needed. One step in making the data comparable, while also developing responses based on them, is the use of an inclusive definition of what 'shrinking space' implies and who the directly affected actors are. As elaborated in paragraph 2, the terms HRD, NGO, and civil society, are highly disputed. To apply a holistic and effective protection approach, it is necessary to agree on common definitions. In this way, it would be possible to identify specific violations in specific situations with the aid of international human rights law. A potential option to overcome this is, for instance, to agree on the definitions provided by the OSCE Guidelines. The OSCE Guidelines, as opposed to the other international documents, offer comprehensive definitions and highlight the place where the norms and rules are based in international law. Through this systematic approach, the OSCE Guidelines contribute to the advancement of equal protection of human rights and especially endeavour to protect "those who are at risk as a result of their human rights work,"[388] namely human rights defenders.

To facilitate a safe and enabling environment, three kinds of strategies can be implemented: promoting human rights at the domestic level through enhancing commitment, institutions and processes; operating through alliances and networks; and strengthening the authority, credibility and legitimacy of HRDs.[389] Building capacities means to make sure that all actors are aware of the rights and tools available to them. This includes education regarding all legal documents, guidelines and training programs – domestic and international.[390] Working through networks and alliances requires the right political, governmental and organizational structures.[391] Strengthening institutions and promoting human rights on all levels also requires the involvement of elected offi-

388 OSCE, Guidelines on the Protection of Human Rights Defenders, p. xi.

389 *Nah, et al.*, A Research Agenda for the Protection of Human Rights Defenders, Journal of Human Rights Practice, Volume 5, Issue 3, p. 413.

390 Ibid.

391 Ibid, p. 414.

cials and other government representatives, as the State generally has the primary task to secure the protection framework.[392] What stands out is that the three identified strategies are closely linked and overlapping. One other salient feature regarding the latter point is the establishment of national human rights institutions (NHRIs). Those institutions may play an important role in the protection of HRDs and organizations. They are established by domestic governments in order to protect and promote human rights and are usually independent in their work.[393] They are – provided that they are actually free and independent – equipped with various competencies such as monitoring violations against HRDs, providing information or legal assistance to HRDs, interacting with domestic and international bodies or receiving and considering complaints by HRDs, as well as monitoring the implementation of the HRD Guidelines and the UN Declaration on human rights defenders.[394] The EU has also recognized this potential and increased its support for NHRIs.[395] It became, for instance, the first measure of the first aim of the EU Action Plan on Human Rights and Democracy 2015–2019.[396]

Another component is strategic litigation elaborated through third party interventions. In a sanction system basically based on a 'naming and shaming' approach – like the international legal system – third party concerns raised by other States, international or supranational bodies, can have a positive effect. A particularly good attempt to express resentments over civil society restrictions and human rights violations in this context is unequivocally the Universal Periodic Review. In the UPR, the UN Human Rights Council reviews all UN Member States with respect to their compliance with, relevant human rights commitments.[397] This is a highly inclusive process, involving States,

392 *Nah, et al.*, A Research Agenda for the Protection of Human Rights Defenders, Journal of Human Rights Practice, Volume 5, Issue 3, p. 413.

393 *Kreienkamp*, Responding to the Global Crackdown on Civil Society, Global Governance Institute, Policy Brief September 2017, p. 11.

394 OSCE, Guidelines on the Protection of Human Rights Defenders, pp. 126 f.

395 Directorate-General for External Policies, Policy Department, Shrinking space for civil society: the EU response, 2017, p. 15.

396 Ibid.

397 *Lochbihler*, Eine Erklärung für die Menschheit – Rückblick und Perspektiven, German Review on the United Nations, Issue 6/2018, p. 247.

civil society actors, NGOs and UN Special Rapporteurs among others.[398] Oppressive States often fear the potential reputational costs of such reviews, even though in many cases for potentially disputable motivations, like international retaliation or economic sanctions.[399] The role of NGOs as litigators before the ECtHR is also part of this approach and has already been analysed in paragraph 3.2.2.4.

Restrictions on funding, as analysed in detail in paragraph 4.1.2, are often underestimated as the degree of violation is perceived to be less intense. The point is crucial, however, because the criticism expressed by States is, to some extent, comprehensible and certainly legitimate. Transparency on the part of NGOs and their funding is critical in two respects. Firstly, States fear interference by foreign interests or the financing of terrorism. Secondly, on the downside, NGOs need to maintain public trust and endorsement in order to ensure that they are the actual spokespersons of the people they assert to represent.[400] It is observable that the link between NGOs and the local population gets weaker the more the organization relies on foreign funding.[401] Hence, NGOs should reassess their funding models and accept transparency interests. This rethinking is fully beneficial for all actors. Governments receive their information (as long as the interests are legitimate and not arbitrary) and the people are included, which ultimately leads to less suspicion on all sides. Possible new options for NGOs could be, for instance, to provide for paid services, to shift to membership models, to consider crowdfunding or to tap into the trend of social entrepreneurship.[402] A best practice example here is the restructuring of Amnesty International within the last years. The centralistic approach was discontinued and more local entities in the relevant regions have been

398 *Lochbihler*, Eine Erklärung für die Menschheit – Rückblick und Perspektiven, German Review on the United Nations, Issue 6/2018, p. 247.

399 *Kreienkamp*, Responding to the Global Crackdown on Civil Society, Global Governance Institute, Policy Brief September 2017, p. 11.

400 Ibid, p. 10.

401 *Mendelson*, Why Governments Target Civil Society and What Can Be Done in Response – A New Agenda, Center for Strategic and International Studies CSIS, 2015, p. 3.

402 *Rekosh*, Rethinking the Human Rights Business Model – New and Innovative Structures and Strategies for Local Impact, Center for Strategic and International Studies CSIS, 2017, p. 7.

established.[403] Furthermore, the funding is mainly secured due to a membership model which connects the people they claim to speak for very closely to the organization. If organizations are willing to renew themselves and States accomplish their duties under international law, such as not restricting funding under the guise of foreign interference, preventing money laundering or simply acting in the national or moral interests, the cohabitation will not only function, but moreover strengthen a vital civil society, benefitting everyone living in it.

It can be stated that a sensitization of all stakeholders regarding the topic must be achieved. The available instruments and documents must be widespread and available for HRDs, as well as for State authorities, including diplomats. If the issue is well known and, for instance, guidelines are provided for diplomatic personnel, a greater protection for HRDs under threat can be reached in the respective countries. Strengthening implementation and enforcement of the United Nations HRD Declaration can, *inter alia*, be promoted through awareness and comprehension of the topic. Being aware of the matter enables stakeholders to detect early warning signals and respond quickly and appropriately. This would, for instance, allow EU Member States to detect restrictive legislation and counteract such laws before they are adopted.

In sum, it is good to know that the issue has constantly gained attention, but it is still important to take actions against it. Through analysing the threats and shortcomings regarding HRDs and civil society, one thing becomes clear, the movement in its entirety remains strikingly resistant, but individual components – primarily HRDs and their organizations – persists at risk.[404] As seen, States exploit such circumstances to impose restrictions on HRDs and establish a hostile climate. Restricting funds, liquidating or attacking an organization, defaming, arbitrarily detaining, or even killing an HRD is no trivial offence. It constitutes an implicit avowal of a larger, structural threat.[405] "Govern-

403 Amnesty International, The Global Transition Programme Roadmap, Internal Issues News No. 26, March 2013, https://www.amnesty.org.uk/files/iin_mar_2013_gtp_0.pdf.

404 *Roth*, The Abuser's Reaction: Intensifying Attacks on Human Rights Defenders, Orgnizations, and Institutions, 16 Brown J. World Aff. 15, 2010, p. 25.

405 Ibid, p. 26.

ments try to silence the messenger because they do not want the message heard."[406]

Using the quite accurate tools provided under the existing legal framework should enable the relevant stakeholders to exceed second-guessing regarding the true purpose behind States' attacks on free civil space.[407] The normative instruments can be used in both directions, to protect HRDs and also to confine the range of permissible measures available to the State, which finally brings structure and clarity to an area often burdened by discussions of politics and advocacy, and the differing interests therein.[408] It is necessary to establish a human rights protection system originating in, and in pursuit of, also governmental interests, as states are the primary duty bearers regarding protective frameworks. This can be achieved through a framework of internationally accepted rules that can finally lead to greater acceptance and advocacy on behalf of vulnerable people and organizations under threat, even when the perpetrator is an ally.[409] This is central to democracies where political or other alliances of interests are subordinate to the legal framework of fundamental rights. Such vibrant democracies are, however, reliant on a viable civil society.[410]

Hence, a comprehensive and holistic approach includes a series of measures ranging from political, institutional, legal and others. Primarily adopting a legal framework, a comprehensive public order and national action plans in order to protect HRDs at risk.[411] Moreover, the acceptance of democratic values, recognition that the entire society benefits from the work of HRDs, and compliance with the internation-

---

406 *Roth*, The Abuser's Reaction: Intensifying Attacks on Human Rights Defenders, Orgnizations, and Institutions, 16 Brown J. World Aff. 15, 2010, p. 26.

407 *Buyse*, Squeezing civic space: restrictions on civil society organizations and the linkage with human rights, The International Journal of Human Rights 2018 Vol. 22, No. 8, p. 982.

408 Ibid.

409 *Roth*, The Abuser's Reaction: Intensifying Attacks on Human Rights Defenders, Orgnizations, and Institutions, 16 Brown J. World Aff. 15, 2010, p. 26.

410 *Kreienkamp*, Responding to the Global Crackdown on Civil Society, Global Governance Institute, Policy Brief September 2017, p. 12.

411 Third Party Intervention by the Council of Europe Commissioner for Human, Application No. 42705/11 Svetlana Khusainovna ESTEMIROVA against the Russian Federation, 14 March 2016, CommDH(2016)18, § 39.

al human rights protection regime should be the foundation of all further steps. Empowering NHRIs and other bodies is equally a part of a comprehensive approach, as much as fully functional appeal bodies and the possibility of an effective legal remedy, and finally, recognition of the legitimate work conducted by HRDs.[412] The HRD Declaration can, in that regard, be seen as the toolbox and its articles as the tools. All the apparent shortcomings, as discussed, and also the answers, are reflected in the document, if it is indeed read in accordance with the international norms depicted in it. Thus, an actual implementation and establishment of effective enforcement mechanisms are the keys to success.

412 Third Party Intervention by the Council of Europe Commissioner for Human, Application No. 42705/11 Svetlana Khusainovna ESTEMIROVA against the Russian Federation, 14 March 2016, CommDH(2016)18, § 39.

# 5 Conclusion

As demonstrated in the study, the issue of shrinking space and its consequences has grown out from a number of occurrences in particular regions, to a worldwide issue.[413] It also became evident that "[t]here can be no guarantee of fundamental freedoms or human rights in a world where human rights defenders continue to be persecuted for their work."[414]

The activity of HRDs and NGOs is not only important, the degree of leeway to work freely and safely is a strong indicator for the overall health of democracy, as well as the place and value of fundamental rights in a country. While the trend goes continuously downwards – as states imitate the authoritarian tendencies of their neighbours – oppressive developments have become more widespread and are tolerated by more and more people. Likewise, however, the awareness and recognition of such devastating patterns has risen. The crucial point is to go beyond the step of just recognizing and naming worrying trends, towards a holistic approach to support and protect HRDs, and to reopen the space for establishing a vital civil society. The present study has shown that one of the main factors in achieving this is to create a safe and enabling environment for HRDs. Having accomplished this, further improvements and enhancements are also possible. If there is a level playing field for HRDs, NGOs and States – with every party concerned is aware of their rights, obligations, duties and responsibilities – each of them can act in accordance with internationally-set standards. To achieve this, it is necessary not only to blame States for their misconduct, states must also be made aware of the benefits of a vital civil society and of collaborating with HRDs and NGOs. Repressive and au-

413 *Buyse*, Squeezing civic space: restrictions on civil society organizations and the linkage with human rights, The International Journal of Human Rights 2018 Vol. 22, No. 8, p. 982.

414 OSCE, Guidelines on the Protection of Human Rights Defenders, p. ix.

thoritarian governance will, in the long term, not secure a peaceful coexistence between governments and the population within a state, a region and finally on a global scale. A real implementation of the UN Declaration on human rights defenders, beyond only confessions of goodwill, must including the introduction of enforcement mechanisms, which would be the most advantageous solution to combat such scenarios. This would be a clear manifestation of compliance with international human rights law and a strengthening of the international human rights protection regime.

The thesis illuminates that shrinking or even closing civil space is no longer just an issue regarding the Global South, it has fully reached the Global North and thus states which were previously democratic. These developments must be confronted before the transformation towards an illiberal society has been completed. To depict this development, a paraphrased version of Niemöller's famous lines,[415] adapted into the present time and place:

> First they came for the migrants, and I did not speak out – because I was not a migrant.
> Then they came for the refugees, and I did not speak out – because I was not a refugee.
> Then they came for the human rights defenders, and I did not speak out – because I was not a human rights defender.
> Then they criminalized and delegitimized non-governmental organizations, and I did not speak out – because I was not a member of such organization.
> Then they came for me and there was no one left to speak for me.

The thing is, simply put, that the matter is urgent. The undermining and criminalization of civil society and their actors affects everyone in the long run. Hence, ongoing analysis of the dimensions and versatile shapes of shrinking or closing space and finding solutions to tackle the phenomenon is essential. It must also be noted, however, that there is no one-size-fits-all solution. "Defending human rights has never been a consensus project and has almost always been the product of strug-

415 Original quote came from the poem "First they came..." by Pastor Martin Niemöller.

gle."[416] All aspects – the national, international or political contexts, the range of limitations enacted, attacks against HRDs, as well as the particular structures and characteristics of NGOs – must be taken into consideration in order to effectively respond to the shortcomings and to establish a greater scale of protection.[417] Thus, a holistic approach must include effective responses with regard to reactions following violations, as well as prevention-oriented policies beforehand. This would not only combat the symptoms but also force back the causes of horrendous violence.

Taking stock of the health human rights protection globally, upon the 70th anniversary of the Universal Declaration of Human Rights and the 20th of the Declaration on human rights defenders, paints a bleak picture. However, the 'endtimes for human rights' mentioned at the beginning of this thesis have not yet materialised. Nevertheless, the spiral heads downwards and thus, advocates for human rights and their organizations must swiftly reconsider several of their presumptions, reevaluate their policies, and expand their extend, while remaining resilient on the fundamental principles.[418] By creatively using all the tools provided in the toolbox of international law, the shrunken, or even closed space for civil society can enlarge anew. The proper response depends on ourselves.

416 *Alston*, Human Rights Under Siege, SUR 25 – v.14n.25, p. 268.
417 *Kreienkamp*, Responding to the Global Crackdown on Civil Society, Global Governance Institute, Policy Brief September 2017, p. 10.
418 *Alston*, Human Rights Under Siege, SUR 25 – v.14n.25, p. 268.

# Bibliography

## Books & Commentaries


| | |
|---|---|
| Bantekas, Ilias / Oette, Lutz | International Human Rights Law and Practice Cambridge University Press, 2nd Edition, 2016 |
| Beer, Christopher Todd / Bartley, Tim / Roberts, Wade T. | NGOs: Between Advocacy, Service Provision and Regulation<br>In: Levi-Faur, David (Ed),The Oxford Handbook of Governance, Oxford University Press, 2012 |
| Bennett, Karen | A Protection Regime in Need of Committed Action: European Union Support for Human Rights Defenders<br>In: Isa Gómez, Felipe / Mugurza Churruca, Cristina, Wouters, Jan (Editors), EU Human Rights and Democratization Policies: Achievements and Challenges, Routledge, 2018 |
| Bowring, Bill | The Crisis of the European Court of Human Rights in the Face of Authoritarian and Populist Regimes<br>In: Kent, Avidan / Trinidad, Jamie / Skoutaris, Nicos (Editors.), The Future of International Courts. Routledge. (Forthcoming)<br>Chapter available at: https://ssrn.com/abstract =3291425 (viewed: 08.01.2019) |
| Calliess, Christian | The Charter of Fundamental Rights of the European Union,<br>In: Ehlers, Dirk (Editor), European Fundamental Rights and Freedoms, De Gruyter, Berlin 2011 |
| Carew, Boulding | NGOs, Political Protest, and Civil Society Cambridge University Press, New York 2014 |

| | |
|---|---|
| Cichowski, Rachel A. | Civil Society and the European Court of Human Rights<br>In: Christoffersen, Jonas / Madsen, Mikael Rask (Editors),The European Court of Human Rights between Law and Politics, Oxford University Press, 2011 |
| De Schutter, Oliver | International Human Rights Law: Cases, Materials, Commentary Cambridge University Press, 2014 |
| De Vylder, Helena | Rewriting CLR on behalf of Valentin Campeanu v Romania (ECtHR): actio popularis as ultimum remedium to enhance access to justice of victims with a mental disability<br>In: Brems, Eva / Desmet, Ellen (Editors), Integrated Human Rights in Practice: Rewriting Human Rights Decisions, Edward Elgar Publishing, 2017 |
| Edwards, Michael | Civil Society, 3rd Edition<br>Polity Press, Cambridge 2014 |
| Forsythe, David P. | Human Rights in International Relations<br>Cambridge University Press, 3rd Edition, New York 2012 |
| Fowler, Alan | Development NGOs<br>In: Edwards, Michael (Editor), The Oxford Handbook of Civil Society, Oxford University Press, 2011 |
| Freedom House | Freedom in the World 2018: The Annual Survey of Political Rights and Civil Liberties, Rowman & Littlefield Publishers, New York, Washington, 2019 |
| | Freedom in the World 2017: The Annual Survey of Political Rights and Civil Liberties, Rowman & Littlefield Publishers, New York, Washington, 2018 |
| Groenleer, Martijn | The Autonomy of European Union Agencies – A Comparative Study of Institutional Development<br>Eburon 2009 |

| | |
|---|---|
| Haddad, Heidi Nichols | The Hidden Hands of Justice: NGOs, Human Rights and International Courts<br>Cambridge University Press, 2018 |
| Harris, David / O'Boyle, Michael / Warbrick, Colin | Law of the European Convention on Human Rights, 4th Edition,<br>Oxford University Press 2018 |
| Heyns, Christof / Killander, Magnus | Universality and the Growth of Regional Systems<br>In: Shelton, Dinah (Editor), The Oxford Handbook of International Human Rights Law, Oxford University Press, 2013 |
| Hicks, Peggy | Human Rights Diplomacy: The NGO Role<br>In: O'Flaherty, Michael / Zdzisław Kędzi / Müller, Amrei / Ulrich, George (Editors), Human Rights Diplomacy: Contemporary Perspectives, Martinus Nijhoff Publishers, Leiden, Boston 2011 |
| Hodson, Loveday | NGOs and the Struggle for Human Rights in Europe<br>Oxford and Portland, Oregon 2011 |
| Hopgood, Stephen | The Endtimes of Human Rights<br>Ithaca: Cornell University Press, 2013 |
| Janis, Mark W. / Kay, Richard S. / Bradley, Anthony W. | European Human Rights Law: Texts and Materials, 3rd Edition, Oxford University Press, 2008 |
| Marauhn, Thilo | Freedom of Expression, Freedom of Assembly and Association,<br>In: Ehlers, Dirk (Editor), European Fundamental Rights and Freedoms, De Gruyter, Berlin 2011 |
| Rainey, Bernadette / Wicks, Elizabeth / Ovey, Clare | Jacobs, White, and Ovey: The European Convention on Human<br>Rights, 7th Edition<br>Oxford University Press, Oxford 2017 |
| Schabas, William A. | The European Convention on Human Rights: A Commentary<br>Oxford Commentaries on International Law, 1st Edition, Oxford<br>2015 |

| | |
|---|---|
| Scholte, Jan Aart | Relations with Civil Society<br>In: Katz Cogan, Jacob / Hurd, Ian / Johnstone, Ian (Editors), The Oxford Handbook of International Organizations, Oxford University Press, Oxford 2016 |
| Terto Neto, Ulisses | Protecting Human Rights Defenders in Latin America – A legal and Socio-Political Analysis of Brazil<br>Palgrave Macmillan, 2018 |
| Thiel, Markus | European Civil Society and Human Rights Advocacy<br>PENN University of Pennsylvania Press, Philadelphia 2017 |
| UN Special Rapporteur on the Situation of Human Rights | Commentary to the Declaration on human rights defenders<br>Available at: https://www.ohchr.org/Documents/Issues/Defenders/CommentarytoDeclarationondefendersjuly2011.pdf (viewed: 01.12.2018) |
| Van Veen, Wino J. M. | Civil Society in Europe and the European Convention on Human Rights<br>In: Van der Ploeg, Tymen J. / van Veen, Wino J. M. / Versteegh, Cornelia R. M. (Editors), Civil Society in Europe: Minimum Norms and Optimum Conditions of its Regulation, Cambridge University Press, 2017 |
| Von Arnauld, Andreas | Völkerrecht, 3rd Edition<br>C. F. Müller, 2016 |
| Weissbrodt, David | Roles and Responsibilities of Non-State Actors<br>In: Shelton, Dinah (Editor), The Oxford Handbook of International Human Rights Law, Oxford University Press, 2013 |
| Zysset, Alain | The ECHR and Human Rights Theory: Reconciling the Moral and the Political Conceptions, Routledge Research in Human Rights Law, London, New York 2017 |

## Journals & Articles


| | |
|---|---|
| Abbott, Kenneth W. / Keohane, Robert O. / Moravcsik, Andrew / Slaughter, Anne-Marie/ Snidal, Duncan | The Concept of Legalization, International Organization Volume 54, Issue 3, Summer 2000, pp. 401–419 |
| Alston, Philip | The Populist Challenge to Human Rights, *Journal of Human Rights Practice*, Volume 9, Issue 1, 1 February 2017, pp. 1–15<br>Human Rights Under Siege, SUR – International Journal on Human Rights, Volume 14, No. 25, pp. 267–272, 2017 |
| Bennett, Karen | European Union Guidelines on Human Rights Defenders: a review of policy and practice towards effective implementation, The International Journal of Human Rights, Vol. 19 No. 7, 2015, pp. 908–934 |
| Bennett, Karen / Ingleton, Danna / Nah, Alice M. / Savage, James | Critical perspectives on the security and protection of human rights defenders, The International Journal of Human Rights, Volume 19 No. 7, pp. 883–895, 2015 |
| Bourke, Tyler J. | The Role of NGOs in the International Human Rights System: A Case Study—IJM in Thailand, Global Tides, Vol. 4, Article 2, 2010 |
| Buyse, Antoine | Squeezing civic space: restrictions on civil society organizations and the linkage with human rights, The International Journal of Human Rights Volume 22, No. 8, pp. 966–988, 2018 |
| Cernov, Ana | Civil Society is not the Enemy<br>Sur – International Journal on Human Rights 26 Volume 14 No. 26, 2017, pp. 49–60 |
| Cliquennois, Gaëtan / Champetier, Brice | The Economic, Judicial and Political Influence Exerted by Private Foundations on Cases Taken by NGOs to the European Court of Human Rights: Inklings of a New Cold War'? European Law Journal, Volume 22, Issue 1, 2016, pp. 92–126 |

| | |
|---|---|
| Eaton, Caitlin | Human Rights Defenders in the United Nations Framework, Human Rights Defender Volume 25 Issue 1, 2016 |
| Fernández, Luis Enrique Eguren / Patel, Champa | Towards developing a critical and ethical approach for better recognising and protecting human rights defenders, The International Journal of Human Rights, Volume 19 No. 7,2015, pp. 896–907 |
| Guluzade, Mahammad / Bourjaily, Natalia | The NGO Law: Azerbaijan Loses Another Case in the European Court *The International Journal of Not-for-Profit Law,* Volume 12, Issue 3, May 2010 http://www.icnl.org/research/journal/vol12iss3/art_2.htm (viewed: 12.12.2018) |
| Kapronczay, Stefánia | War on NGOs in Eastern Europe, SUR – International Journal on Human Rights 26, Volume 14, No. 26, 2017, pp. 109–118 |
| Kiai, Maina | Reclaiming Civic Space through U.N. Supported Litigation, SUR – International Journal on Human Rights 22 – Volume 12 No. 22, 2015, pp. 245–251 |
| Lochbihler, Barbara | Eine Erklärung für die Menschheit – Rückblick und Perspektiven VEREINTE NATIONEN, Zeitschrift für die Vereinten Nationen und ihre Sonderorganisationen (German Review on the United Nations), Heft 6, 2018, pp. 243–248 |
| Martens, Kerstin | Examining the (Non-)Status of NGOs in International Law, Indiana Journal of Global Legal Studies, Volume 10, Issue 2, Article 1, 2003 |
| Merle, Marcel | International Non-governmental Organizations and their Legal Status, Appendix 3.5 of the International Associations Statutes Series Volume 1, UIA eds, 1988 https://uia.org/archive/legal-status-3-5 (viewed: 10.11.2018) |

| | |
|---|---|
| Nah, Alice M. / Bennett, Karen / Ingleton, Danna / Savage, James | A Research Agenda for the Protection of Human Rights Defenders, *Journal of Human Rights Practice*, Volume 5, Issue 3, 1 November 2013, pp. 401–420 |
| Roth, Kenneth | The Abuser's Reaction: Intensifying Attacks on Human Rights Defenders, Orgnizations, and Institutions, The Brown Journal of World Affairs, Volume XVI, Issue II, 2010 |
| Rutzen, Douglas | Civil Society under Assault Journal of Democracy, Volume 26 Number. 4, October 2015, pp. 28–39 |
| Steiner, Nils D. | Comparing Freedom House Democracy Scores to Alternative Indices and Testing for Political Bias: Are US Allies Rated More Democratic by Freedom House? Journal of Comparative Policy Analysis: Research and Practice Volume 18, Issue 4, 2014, pp. 329–349 |
| Thiel, Markus | European Civil Society and the EU Fundamental Rights Agency: Creating Legitimacy through Civil Society Inclusion? Journal of European Integration, Vol. 36, Issue 5, pp. 435–451, 2014 |
| Unmüßig, Barbara | Civil society under pressure – shrinking – closing – no space Heinrich Böll Foundation, Berlin, May 2016 https://www.boell.de/sites/default/files/uploads/2015/12/20160601_civil_socieity_under_pressure_shrinking_spaces_englisch.pdf (viewed: 10.10.2018) |
| Van der Vet, Freek | Transitional Justice in Chechnya: NGO Political Advocacy for Implementing Chechen Judgments of the European Court of Human Rights, Review of Central and East European Law 38, January 2013, pp. 363–388 |

Van der Vet, Freek / Lyytikäinenb, Laura — Violence and human rights in Russia: how human rights defenders develop their tactics in the face of danger, 2005–2013, The International Journal of Human Rights, Volume 19, No. 7,2015, pp. 979–998


## Official & Legal Documents and Policy Papers


African Commission on Human and Peoples' Rights — Kigali Declaration of 8 May 2003, http://www.achpr.org/instruments/kigali/ (viewed: 18.11.2018)

Grand Bay Declaration and Plan of Action, 16 April 1999, http://www.achpr.org/instrument s/grandbay/ (viewed: 18.11.2018)

Amnesty International — Weathering the Storm – Defending Human Rights in Turkey's climate of fear, AI Index: EUR 44/8200/2018, 26 April 2018 https://ww w.amnesty.org/download/Documents/EUR44 82002018ENGLISH.PDF (viewed: 15.11.2018)

Rule without law: Human rights violations in the North Caucasus, AI Index: EUR 46/012/2009, July 2009 https://www.amnesty.org/download/Docume nts/48000/eur460122009en.pdf (viewed: 10.12.2018)

CIVICUS — People Power Under Attack – A Global Analysis of Threats to Fundamental Freedoms, November 2018 https://www.civicus.org/documents/PeoplePo werUnderAttack.Report.27November.pdf (viewed: 02.01.2019)

Consortium PARTICIP-ADE–DIE–DRN-ECDPM-ODI — Thematic evaluation of the European Commission support to respect of Human Rights and Fundamental Freedoms, Final Report Vol. 1, December 2011

| | |
|---|---|
| | https://ec.europa.eu/europeaid/sites/devco/files/evaluation-cooperation-ec-human-rights-1298-main-report-201112_en_0.pdf (viewed: 12.11.2018) |
| Council of Europe | Legal status of non-governmental organisations in Europe Recommendation CM/Rec(2007)14 adopted by the Committee of Ministers of the Council of Europe on 10 October 2007 and explanatory memorandum https://rm.coe.int/16807096b7 (viewed: 05.11.2018) |
| | Declaration of the Committee of Ministers on Council of Europe action to improve the protection of human rights defenders and promote their activities, 6 February 2008, Adopted by the Committee of Ministers at the 1017th meeting of the Ministers' Deputies |
| | *European Convention* on the Recognition of the Legal Personality of International Non-Governmental Organisations, ETS No 124, 24.IV.1986 https://www.coe.int/en/web/conventions/full-list/-/conventions/treaty/124/signatures?p_auth=QFeq77Fy (viewed: 11.01.2019) |
| | Protocol No. 11 to the Convention for the Protection of Human Rights and Fundamental Freedoms, restructuring the control machinery established thereby, ETS No.155 |
| Council of Europe Commissioner for Human Rights | Third Party Intervention by the Council of Europe Commissioner for Human Rights under Article 36 paragraph 3 of the European Convention on Human Rights Application no. 9988/13, Ecodefence and others against Russia and 48 other applications, 5 July 2017 |

| | |
|---|---|
| Council of Europe Commissioner for Human Rights | Third Party Intervention by the Council of Europe Commissioner for Human Rights under Article 36 of the European Convention on Human Rights Application No. 42705/11 Svetlana Khusainovna ESTEMIROVA against the Russian Federation, CommDH(2016)18, 14 March 2016 |
| | Opinion of the Commissioner for Human Rights, Legislation and Practice in the Russian Federation on Non-Commercial Organisations in Light of Council of Europe Standards: an Update, CommDH(2015)17, 9 July 2015 https://rm.coe.int/16806da772 (viewed: 09.01.2019) |
| | Opinion of the Commissioner for Human Rights on the Legislation of the Russian Federation on Non-Commercial Organisations in Light of Council of Europe Standards, CommDH(2013) 15, 15 July 2013 https://rm.coe.int/opinion-of-the-commissioner-for-human-rights-on-the-legislation-of-the/16806da5b2 (viewed: 09.01.2019) |
| Council of Europe Parliamentary Assembly | PACE Resolution 2095, Strengthening the protection and role of human rights defenders in Council of Europe member States, 28 January 2016 |
| | PACE Recommendation 2085, Strengthening the protection and role of human rights defenders in Council of Europe member States, 28 January 2016 |
| | PACE Resolution 1891, The situation of human rights defenders in Council of Europe member States, 27 June 2012 |
| | PACE Resolution 1660, Situation of human rights defenders in Council of Europe member states, 28 April 2009 |

| | |
|---|---|
| Council of Europe Committee of Ministers | Rules of the Committee of Ministers for the supervision of the execution of judgements and of the terms of friendly settlements, adopted by the Committee of Ministers on 10 May 2006 at the $964^{th}$ meeting of the Ministers' Deputies and amended on 18 January 2017 at the $1275^{th}$ meeting of the Ministers' Deputies, https://rm.coe.int/16806eebf0 (viewed: 15.12.2018) |
| Council of the European Union | Official Journal of the European Union, Council Regulation (EC) No 168/2007 of 15 February 2007 |
| | European Union, Ensuring Protection – European Union Guidelines on Human Rights Defenders, 14 June 2004, 10056/1/04 |
| European Commission, Baranowska et al. | EU human rights engagement in UN bodies, Work Package No. 5 – Deliverable No. 5.1, 10.7404/FRAME.REPS. 5.1, 30 November 2014 |
| European Commission for Democracy through Law (Venice Commission) | Venice Commission, Hungary: Opinion on the Draft Law on the Transparency of Organisations Receiving Support from Abroad, CDL-REF(2017)015, 20 June 2017 https://www.venice.coe.int/webforms/documents/default.aspx?pdffile=CDL-AD(2017)015-e (viewed: 09.01.2019) |
| | Opinion on "Law on Foreign Agents" and "Law on Treason" of the Russian Federation, Adopted by the Venice Commission at its $99^{th}$ Plenary Session, CDL-AD(2014)025, 27 June 2014 https://www.venice.coe.int/webforms/documents/default.aspx?pdffile=cdl-ad(2014)025-e (viewed: 09.01.2019) |

| | |
|---|---|
| European Parliament | Directorate-General for External Policies, Policy Department, Shrinking space for civil society: the EU response, April 2017 http://www.europarl.europa.eu/RegData/etudes/STUD/2017/578039/EXPO_STU(2017)578039_EN.pdf (viewed: 28.11.2018) |
| Freedom House | Freedom in the World 2018 Democracy in Crisis, https://freedomhouse.org/sites/default/files/FH_FITW_Report_2018_Final_SinglePage.pdf (viewed: 10.12.2018) |
| Group of Eight | G8 Declaration on Preventing Sexual Violence in Conflict, https://www.un.org/ruleoflaw/files/G8%20Declaration%20Sexual%20Violence%20in%20Conflict%20-%20April%202013.pdf (viewed: 10.10.2018) |
| Human Rights Watch | World Report 2017, Roth, Kenneth: The Dangerous Rise of Populism https://www.hrw.org/sites/default/files/world_report_download/wr2017-web.pdf (viewed: 10.11.2018) |
| International Commission of Jurists (ICJ) and Amnesty International | Third Party Intervention, Written Submissions on Behalf of the International Commission of Jurists (ICJ) and Amnesty International Application no. 9988/13, Ecodefence and others against Russia and 48 other applications, 2 October 2017, https://www.icj.org/wp-content/uploads/2017/10/Russia-ECtHR-AmicusBrief-Ecodefence-legalsubmissions-2017-ENG.pdf (viewed: 10.11.2018) |
| Kinzelbach, Katrin | Ohne Demokratie keine Menschenrechte und kein Frieden, Peace Lab, 12 January 2017 https://peacelab.blog/2017/01/ohne-demokratie-keine-menschenrechte-und-kein-frieden (viewed: 05.01.2019) |

| | |
|---|---|
| Kreienkamp, Julia | Responding to the Global Crackdown on Civil Society, Global Governance Institute, Policy Brief September 2017 https://www.ucl.ac.uk/global-governance/sites/global-governance/files/policy-brief-civil-society.pdf (viewed: 09.01.2019) |
| Mendelson, Sarah E. | Why Governments Target Civil Society and What Can Be Done in Response – A New Agenda, A Report of the CSIS Human Rights Initiative, Center for Strategic and International Studies CSIS, April 2015 https://csis-prod.s3.amazonaws.com/s3fs-public/legacy_files/files/publication/150422_Mendelson_GovTargetCivilSociety_Web.pdf (viewed: 09.01.2019) |
| Organisation for Security and Co-operation in Europe (OSCE) | Dublin Declaration – Security of human rights defenders: time for OSCE to act, Dublin, 5 December 2012, http://www.civicsolidarity.org/ sites/default/files/dublin_declaration_on_human_rights_defenders_final.pdf (viewed: 11.12.2018) |
| | CSCE Budapest Document 1994, Towards a Genuine Partnership in a New Era, https://www.osce.org/mc/39554?download=true (viewed: 01.12.2018) |
| | Document of the Copenhagen Meeting of the Conference on the Human Dimension of the CSCE, Copenhagen 1990 https://www.osce.org/odihr/19394?download=true (viewed: 10.12.2018) |
| | Conference on Security and Co-Operation in Europe Final Act (Helsinki Final Act), Helsinki 1975, https://www.osce.org/helsinki-final-act?download=true (viewed: 15.12.2018) |

| | |
|---|---|
| Organization of American States – General Assembly | OEA/Ser.PAG/RES. 1818 (XXXI-O/01), 5 June 2001, Human Rights Defenders in the Americas |
| OSCE Office for Democratic Institutions and Human Rights (ODIHR) | OSCE Human Dimension Commitments, Volume 1, Thematic Compilation, 2nd Edition, 2005 https://www.osce.org/odihr/elections/16363?download=true (viewed: 14.12.2018) |
| | Independent Civil Society Under Attack in Hungary – Statement by Hungarian NGOs, 22 September 2017 https://www.osce.org/odihr/339316?download=true (viewed: 15.10.2018) |
| | OSCE, Guidelines on the Protection of Human Rights Defenders, 10 June 2014 https://www.osce.org/odihr/guidelines-on-the-protection-of-human-rights-defenders?download=true (viewed: 01.12.2018) |
| Protection International | Legislators and Human Rights Defenders, 2011 https://www.protectioninternational.org/wp-content/uploads/2013/08/Parliamentary-Guide_EN.pdf (viewed: 20.12.2018) |
| Quintana, María Martín / Fernández, Luis Enrique Eguren | Protection of human rights defenders: Best practices and lessons learnt, Protection International 2012 https://www.protectioninternational.org/wp-content/uploads/2013/04/Best-Practices-and-Lessons-Learnt.pdf (viewed: 08.01.2019 |
| Rekosh, Edwin | Rethinking the Human Rights Business Model – New and Innovative Structures and Strategies for Local Impact<br>A Report of the CSIS Human Rights Initiative, Center for Strategic and International Studies CSIS, June 2017<br>https://csis-prod.s3.amazonaws.com/s3fs-public/publication/170614_Rekosh_HumanRightsBusinessModel_Web.pdf?TmI1omXjPrr98zPb (viewed: 08.01.2019) |

| | |
|---|---|
| Transnational Institute, Hayes, et al. | On "shrinking space" – a framing paper , Twomey, Hannah (Editor), Amsterdam, April 2017 https://www.tni.org/files/publication-downloads/on_shrinking_space_2.pdf (viewed: 04.01.2019) |
| UN Commission on Human Rights | E/CN.4/RES/2000/61, 26 April 2000, Human rights defenders |
| UN Economic and Social Council | E/RES/1996/31, Consultative relationship between the United Nations and non-governmental organizations |
| UN General Assembly | A/69/259, 5 August 2014, Report of the UN Special Rapporteur on the Situation of Human Rights Defenders |
| | A/RES/68/181, 18 December 2013, protecting women human rights defenders |
| | A/RES/53/144, Declaration on the Right and Responsibility of Individuals, Groups and Organs of Society to Promote and Protect Universally Recognized Human Rights and Fundamental Freedoms, 8 March 1999, Adopted by General Assembly resolution 53/144 of 9 December 1998 |
| UN Human Rights Committee | General Comment No. 34 on Article 19, CCPR/C/GC/34 |

| | |
|---|---|
| UN Human Rights Council | A/HRC/RES/27/31, 3 October 2014, Civil Society Space |
| | A/HRC/27/L.27/Rev.1, 24 September 2014, resolution on Human Rights, Sexual Orientation and Gender Identity |
| | A/HRC/25/55, 23 December 2013<br>Report of the Special Rapporteur on the situation of human rights defenders, |
| | A/HRC/RES/24/21, 9 October 2013, Civil Society Space |
| | A/HRC/23/39, 24 April 2013 Report of the Special Rapporteur on the rights to freedom of peaceful assembly and of association, Maina Kiai |
| | A/HRC/RES/22/6,12 April 2013, Protecting Human Rights Defenders |
| | A/HRC/RES/7/8, 27 March 2008, Human Rights Council resolution, Mandate of the Special Rapporteur on the situation of human rights defenders |
| UN Office of the High Commissioner for Human Rights (OHCHR) | Fact Sheet No. 29, Human Rights Defenders: Protecting the Right to Defend Human Rights, April 2004, No. 29 |
| Union of International Associations | Law of 25th October 1919 on International Associations with Scientific Objectives, https://uia.org/belgianlaw (viewed: 05.12.2018) |

| | |
|---|---|
| UN Special Rapporteur on the Rights to Freedom of Peaceful Assembly and of Associations and The Human Rights Centre of Ghent University | Joint Third Party Intervention by The United Nations Special Rapporteur on the Rights to Freedom of Peaceful Assembly and of Associations and The Human Rights Centre of Ghent University, Mahammad Majidli v. Azerbaijan (no. 3) and three other applications application Nos. 56317/11, 67932/11, 27472/12 and 59661/12 http://www.hrc.ugent.be/wp-content/uploads/2015/11/Majidli_tpi.pdf (viewed: 05.01.2019) |
| World Economic Forum | The Global Risks Report, 12th Edition, Geneva 2017 http://www3.weforum.org/docs/GRR17_Report_web.pdf (viewed: 05.01.2019) |
| Wouters, Jan / Hermez, Marta | EU Guidelines on Human Rights As a Foreign Policy Instrument: An Assessment, CLEER Papers 2016/5, The Hague, Centre for the Law of EU External Relations, Working Paper No. 170, February 2016 |
| Wouters, Jan / Rossi, Ingrid | Human Rights NGOs: Role, Structure and Legal Status, K.U. Leuven, Institute for International Law Working Paper No 14, 21 November 2001 |

## Internet Sources


| | |
|---|---|
| Amnesty International | Hungary: NGO law a vicious and calculated assault on civil society Press Release, 13 June 2017 https://www.amnesty.org/en/latest/news/2017/06/hungary-ngo-law-a-vicious-and-calculated-assault-on-civil-society/ (viewed: 10.11.2018) The Global Transition Programme Roadmap, Internal Issues News No. 26, March 2013, https://www.amnesty.org.uk/files/iin_mar_2013_gtp_0.pdf (viewed: 10.01.2019) |
| Bustos, Camila | The Shrinking of Civic Spaces: What is Happening and What Can We Do? Dejustica, 17 April 2017 https://www.dejusticia.org/en/column/the-shrinking-of-civic-spaces-what-is-happening-and-what-can-we-do/ (viewed: 06.01.2019) |
| CIVICUS | CIVICUS, Monitor 2016, https://monitor.civicus.org/newsfeed/2016/09/01/united-kingdom-overview/ (viewed: 05.12.2018) |
| | CIVICUS, Monitor 2016, https://monitor.civicus.org/newsfeed/2016/09/01/france-overview/ (viewed: 05.12.2018) |
| Gardner, Andrew | At the Funeral of Tahir Elci a giant in Turkey's Human Rights Movement, the sense of loss is deafening, 30 November 2015 https://www.amnesty.org/en/latest/news/2015/11/at-the-funeral-of-tahir-elci-a-giant-in-turkeys-human-rights-movement-the-sense-of-loss-is-deafening/ (viewed: 10.10.2018) |
| Lawyers of the Committee for Human Rights | Protecting Human Rights Defenders Analysis of the newly adopted Declaration on Human Rights Defenders, *The International Journal of Not-for-Profit Law*, Volume 1, Issue 3, March 1999 http://www.icnl.org/research/journal/vol1iss3/rev.htm#2 (viewed: 11.10.2018) |

| | |
|---|---|
| Stockholm Center for Freedom | Turkish gov't covers up killing of lawyer, human rights activist Tahir Elçi, https://stockholmcf.org/turkish-govt-covers-up-killing-of-lawyer-human-rights-activist-tahir-elci/ (viewed: 18.11.2018) |
| The Nobel Peace Prize 2012 | The Nobel Peace Prize 2012. NobelPrize.org. Nobel Media AB 2019 https://www.nobelprize.org/prizes/peace/2012/summary/ (viewed: 18.11.2018) |
| Yeginsu, Ceylan | Prominent Kurdish Lawyer Is Killed in Southeast Turkey, The New York Times, 28 November 2015, https://www.nytimes.com/2015/11/29/world/europe/turkey-kurds-tahir-elci-killed-in-sur.html (viewed: 12.11.2018) |

# Table of Cases

*Alikhadzhiyeva v. Russia*, no. 68007/01, judgement of 5 July 2007

*Aliyev and others v. Azerbaijan* no. 28736/05, *judgement of 18 December 2008*

*Association for the Defence of Human Rights in Romania – Helsinki Committee on behalf of Ionel Garcea v. Romania*, no. 2959/11, judgement of 24. March 2015

*Djavit An v. Turkey*, no. 20652/92, § 56, ECHR 2003-III

*Ecodefence and others against Russia and 48 other applications*, Application no. 9988/13, Communicated on 22 March 2017

*Estemirova v. Russia*, no. 42705/11, lodged on 21 June 2011, statement of facts

*Gorzelik and Others v. Poland* [GC], no. 44158/98, ECHR 2004-I

*GRA Stiftung gegen Rassismus und Antisemitismus v. Switzerland* no. 18597/13, judgement of 09 January 2018

*Heliodoro Portugal vs Panama*, Series C No. 186, Inter-American Court of Human Rights (IACrtHR), Preliminary Objections, Merits, Reparations and Costs, judgment of August 12, 2008

*Ismayilov v. Azerbaijan* no. 4439/0, judgement of 17 January 2008

*Kondrulin v. Russia*, no. 12987/15, judgement of 30 January 2017

Mahammad Majidli v. Azerbaijan (no. 3) and three other applications application Nos. 56317/11, 67932/11, 27472/12 and 59661/12, Communicated on 2 July 2015

*Mahammad Majidli v. Azerbaijan application* Applications Nos. 24508/11 and 44581/13, judgement of 16 February 2017

*Makayeva v. Russia*, no. 37287/09, judgement of 18 September 2014

*Musayeva and Others v. Russia*, no. 74239/01, judgement of 26 July 2007

*Myrna Mack vs Guatemala*, Series C No. 101, Inter-American Court of Human Rights (IACrtHR), judgement of 25 November 2003

*Nasibova v. Azerbaijan* no. 4307/04, judgement of 18 October 2007

*Ramazanova and Others v. Azerbaijan* no. 44363/02, judgement of 1 February 2007

*Refah Partisi (the Welfare Party) and Others v. Turkey* [GC] no. 41340/98, 41342/98, 41343/98 et al.

*Sidiropoulos and Others v. Greece* [GC], 10 July 1998, § 40, Reports of Judgments and Decisions 1998-IV

*Socialist Party and Others v. Turkey* [GC], judgment of 25 May 1998, Reports 1998-III

Zeitfracht Medien GmbH
Ferdinand-Jühlke-Straße 7
99095 Erfurt, Deutschland
produktsicherheit@kolibri360.de